Gandhi's Jesus

Rational Inspiration for the
Reluctant Animal Rights Activist

Volume III:

Rational Bible Series

Brian S. Whaley

"We cannot have peace among men whose hearts find delight in killing any living creature."

\- Rachel Carson

ISBN-13: 978-0692405826

ISBN-10: 0692405828 :

DEDICATION

I dedicate this book to Jayden, Cadence, Bryce, Brianna, Jessi, and Michael.

Love and truth are eternal!

CONTENTS

Contents

ACKNOWLEDGMENTS

I owe a huge thanks to Michelle Pierson who inspired me at critical times over the course of this endeavor. The same can be said of John and Ann Rush whose transcriptions of their inspiring discussions with Mildred Ryder (the other Peace Pilgrim) inspired me when I needed it most. There were times when I doubted that anyone other than Gandhi could live according to the radical moral precepts so perfectly demonstrated by Jesus. Mildred Ryder, is one of the more recent sojourners of truth, whom having relinquished all her possessions began a 40 year pilgrimage on foot with nothing but the clothing on her back, all in the name of peace.

While inevitable typos and grammatical errors remain, there is no denying that this book is the result of the hard work and generous efforts of numerous proofreaders over the course of the final week. No doubt, many suggestions which have gone unaddressed in this first edition, will be utilized in later prints. I would like to express my deepest gratitude to the Gandhi Research Foundation in Jalgaon. Their painstakingly thorough anthology of Gandhi's writings greatly enhanced my understanding of his philosophy.

Of course, I would be amiss not to acknowledge my readers whom inspire me the most! I believe we are kindred spirits. The fact that you're reading this is an indication that the same Truth that beaconed Gandhi, Tolstoy, Mildred Ryder, Martin Luther King, and Nelson Mandela calls out to you. My only hope is that this book encourages you to act.

Preface

On January 1st of 2013, I woke with a mission. I was to write a book of a spiritual but nonreligious nature. One that would center around the eclipsing effects of narcissism on empathy. At the time, it seemed as if every other self-help book harkened the praises of high self-esteem. "The problem isn't a low opinion of self", I suddenly realized "it's a general disregard of others." One expects to find happiness perched on the higher rungs of social status. But the world is full of over inflated egos, concerned only with preserving their place in a long and purposeless pecking order. Inevitably, someone younger, prettier, stronger or smarter will come along. Other than the preservation of one's name (given at birth) and a few inaccurate myths, even what value is a personal legacy?

At first, I wanted to avoid any mention of scripture. I couldn't stomach the risk of bringing yet another book of unfounded and fantastical superstitions into the world. I wanted hard proof as to the power of a given philosophy for creating lasting change; not only for the individual adherent, but for the whole of society. Now that's a pretty tall order by anyone's standard. For obvious reasons, I felt inclined to study the life and works of Mohandas Gandhi. Not only did he walk his talk, the results of his "experiments with truth" have been replicated by some of history's most renowned agents of social change.

Despite my initial inclinations however, I put off the study of Gandhi's manuscripts. For several months, I scoured the latest research articles, particularly in search of studies on brain imaging, addiction, codependency, happiness, and empathy. The result of those efforts are various volumes of nearly complete manuscripts. Each one a little closer to the truth; just shy of a viable philosophy for creating meaningful and purposeful change.

Obviously, I did get around to reading the memoirs of Gandhi. In retrospect, my previous efforts seemed akin to holding one's thumb over a water spigot. My intentions had been pure and my efforts forceful, but I lacked purpose-filled direction. One that would keep me up at night and haunt the inkling of my dreams.

When I finally tired of doing things my own way, I turned to Gandhi's autobiography, "The Story of My Experiments With truth." With every turn of the page, I felt strangely validated. The experience was akin to one of those cartoon characters with their temples popped out of their heads (accentuated by the sound of a train whistle). Immediately, my thoughts and observations resonated with Gandhi. I had goosebumps for days with every cell in my body screaming, "Don't let this truth slip away!" It was as if I'd spent my entire life either asleep or fumbling around in the dark.

What made the greatest initial impression on me, was Gandhi's admiration of Tolstoy, a Russian novelist best known for fictional works like, "War and Peace" and "Anna Karenina." These novels are considered by many, to be among the greatest works of literature ever produced. Yet the older, morally convicted Tolstoy renounced the copyrights to these works, as having no significance for the plight of the common Man. It was of course, his subsequent works, specifically "The Kingdom of God Is Within You" that so greatly affected Gandhi. Tolstoy's interpretation of the Gospels cemented for me also, the foundations of my personal philosophy and the basis of this book.

I touch on the intricacies of Gandhi and Tolstoy's relationship throughout the introduction and body of this book. The purpose of my writing this preface however, is simply to explain the relationship between activism, animal rights and the teachings of Jesus. I believe that every person was born with an innate fondness for the companionship of nonhuman animals. Early in life however, we learn to barter even our most precious gift and spend the remainder in search of it. Perhaps we even forgotten what "it" is; the source of life's original sense of wonder. Without compassion, living things become objects to be exploited for other objects (food, sex, money etc.). No wonder we feel dead inside. Without love and compassion, the human experience is void of life.

Throughout this book, I refer to "the call of the Spirit" or the "Holy Ghost." Other times I call it "truth", "love", "empathy" "compassion" or "the voice of conscience." In matriarchal and patriarchal societies they call it respectfully "the Mother" or "the Father." In virtually every society however, it is revered as the *source of life*. Call it what you will, just don't get turned off by the sometimes unavoidably pious semantics you are sure to encounter throughout this book. But rest assured, I wrote this book for the critical thinker because I know the frustration of being drawn to the Bible, only to stumble upon its many contradictions.

Trust me on this one, the core of Jesus' philosophy is both viable and revolutionary. But most rational minded folks miss it for the misguided attempts of primeval stakeholders to deify him. Jesus was a relentless activist. But he wasn't perfect and he wasn't "God." Jesus makes this clear in Matthew[19:17] as he quotes Hannah's prayer which can be found in 1st Samuel.[2:2] Virtually everything that Jesus is recorded to have said and done was an act ceaseless prayer. Well, there are exceptions, like Mark[11:12-14] where Jesus eagerly approaches a fig tree hoping to find fruit but finding only leaves, he curses it! Mark cheekfully notes that figs were out of season. That is one of my favorite verses because it validates the account as one having reminisced of an old and dear friend.

Of course each of the Bible verses can and should be viewed as moral allegory. The NT's reoccurring references to the barren fruit tree can be employed as a parable referencing the futility of fruitless forms of worship and the need for relentless activism. The author of 2nd Timothy references it in just this way.

"Preach the word; be instant in season, out of season; reprove, rebuke, exhort with all longsuffering and doctrine." –2 Timothy 4:2

Only when subjective interpretations are taken to the literal extreme, does the Bible become a political machine of social division and deceit. In Matthew 15:1-24 Jesus is quoted to have said, "Listen to this and understand: it is not that which goes into the mouth which defiles a man, but that which comes out." For obvious reasons this passage caused a major rift between the vegetarian and meat-eating sects of the early Christian church. (Sadly, the most common use of the Bible seems only to justify immoral behavior). When the passage is read in full with a rational mind however, we see that Jesus' hasty reply was given in response to religionist scorn. Turns out, the disciple's weren't in the habit of washing their hands before sitting down to eat! Once again, we find reference to a more believable, relatable beautifully imperfect, mortal Jesus.

According to the preceding passage, Jesus and his disciples weren't privy to the hygienic value of washing one's hands before eating. Not surprisingly, Jesus' disciples drew him aside asking "Do you not realize that you offended the Pharisees by what you said back there?" Such a response is meant to point out that Jesus, (incensed by the religionists) broke his own mandate not to "resist an evil." Again, I find great joy in such passages because it <u>authenticates for me</u>, the more relatable humanity of Jesus. It is perfectly natural that we should edify our teachers, but we shouldn't put them so high on a pedestal that we lose all reason and faculty for rational thought.

Had he identified himself as a Christian, Gandhi himself would have been contorted a Saint. He is referred to as "Mahatma" (Sanskrit for "great soul") more often in fact, than his given name of "Mohandas." In India, he is referred to simply as "Bapu" which in Gujarati is a term of endearment for "father." Get where I'm going with this? Lasting faith is founded firmly on reason, not fanatical adulation. In my research on Gandhi and his writings, I encountered multiple racial slurs and inconsistent comments. But Gandhi was just a man, no "greater" than the rest of us. To believe otherwise is to set oneself up for disappointment. We learn from our own mistakes. Shouldn't we allow our teachers the same privilege?

Jesus' detractors were no different from Gandhi's in that they were bent on destruction, not truth.

"Blessed are the poor in spirit: for theirs is the kingdom of heaven. Blessed are they that mourn: for they shall be comforted. Blessed are the meek: for they shall inherit the earth. Blessed are they which do hunger and thirst after righteousness: for they shall be filled. Blessed are the merciful: for they shall obtain mercy. Blessed are the pure in heart: for they shall see God. Blessed are the peacemakers: for they shall be called the children of God. Blessed are they which are persecuted for righteousness' sake: for *theirs is the kingdom of heaven.* Blessed are ye, when men shall revile you, and persecute you, and shall say all manner of evil against you falsely, for my sake. Rejoice, and be exceeding glad: for *great is your reward in heaven:* for so persecuted they the prophets which were before you. Ye are the salt of the earth: but if the salt have lost his savour, wherewith shall it be salted? it is thenceforth good for nothing, but to be cast out, and to be trodden under foot of men. Ye are the light of the world. A city that is set on an hill cannot be hid. Neither do men light a candle, and put it under a bushel, but on a candlestick; and it giveth light unto all that are in the house. Let your light so shine before men, that they may see your good works, and glorify your Father which is in heaven.

–Matthew 5:3-16

"Blessed are ye, when men shall hate you, and when they shall separate you from their company, and shall reproach you, and cast out your name as evil, for the Son of man's sake. Rejoice ye in that day, and leap for joy: for, behold, your reward is great in heaven: for in the like manner did their fathers unto the prophets."

-Luke 6.22-23

Take <u>Your</u> Time

When we idolize our teachers we tend to adopt everything they profess to believe. I often refer to this phenomenon as "willful blindness." But anyone who speaks to the truth can expect their inadequacies to be brought to light. And just as sure as good things start to happen, the vultures will come. The ones found spiritually dead on the wayside are the followers whose faith wasn't grounded on solid reason. That's why it's so important to become good stewards of our time. Corporations have an economical basis for paying out trillions of dollars in advertising each year and it's not to entertain. Our time is the most valuable limited resource we have. Please tune out the media, and take back your time! Start developing your own personal philosophy founded firmly on reason. Write your criticisms, corrections and additional insights in the margins of this book, and don't forget to share them with me (personal@brianwhaley.com).

"He is like a man which built an house, and digged deep, and laid the foundation on a rock: and when the flood arose, the stream beat vehemently upon that house, and could not shake it: for it was founded upon a rock. But he that heareth, and doeth not, is like a man that without a foundation built an house upon the earth; against which the stream did beat vehemently, and immediately it fell; and the ruin of that house was great."

–Luke 6:48-49

"Therefore whosoever heareth these sayings of mine, and doeth them, I will liken him unto a wise man, which built his house upon a rock: And the rain descended, and the floods came, and the winds blew, and beat upon that house; and it fell not: for it was founded upon a rock. And every one that heareth these sayings of mine, and doeth them not, shall be likened unto a foolish man, which built his house upon the sand: And the rain descended, and the floods came, and the winds blew, and beat upon that house; and it fell: and great was the fall of it."

–Matthew 7:24-27

"Every wise woman buildeth her house: but the foolish plucketh it down with her hands. He that walketh in his uprightness feareth the LORD: but he that is perverse in his ways despiseth him. In the mouth of the foolish is a rod of pride: but the lips of the wise shall preserve them. Where no oxen are, the crib is clean: but much increase is by the strength of the ox. A faithful witness will not lie: but a false witness will utter lies. A scorner seeketh wisdom, and findeth it not: but knowledge is easy unto him that understandeth. Go from the presence of a foolish man, when thou perceivest not in him the lips of knowledge. The wisdom of the prudent is to understand his way: but the folly of fools is deceit. Fools make a mock at sin: but among the righteous there is favour. The heart knoweth his own bitterness; and a stranger doth not intermeddle with his joy. The house of the wicked shall be overthrown: but the tabernacle of the upright shall flourish. There is a way which seemeth right unto a man, but the end thereof are the ways of death. Even in laughter the heart is sorrowful; and the end of that mirth is heaviness. The backslider in heart shall be filled with his own ways: and a good man shall be satisfied from himself. The simple believeth every word: but the prudent man looketh well to his going.

–Proverbs 14:1–15

I know this book is one of many you have read in hopes of discovering some sustenance of truth that will give your life a semblance of truth and purpose. But NO book can do that. The best I can hope for is to help you uncover and confirm what God has already placed within you. (If you're an atheist, your safe to keep reading also, my God is truth. As was Gandhi's.) Even still, reading this book in its entirety will take some forging on your behalf. As an author, as in every area of my life, I am a work in progress. Just consider it an exercise in unconditional love on your part. That is, don't reject the message on account of the messenger which is what I did for the better part of my life. While growing up, my mother had me in church at least three times a week. Needless to say, I passed a lot of notes and I don't even want to think about all the ceiling tiles I've counted. Even as a child, I was bored with the Bible's many fantastical tales because the preacher presented them as fact rather than fable.

Rational minded folks have little patience for the Bible's talking donkeys, satyrs, unicorns, cockatrices and dragons. But the Bible records for posterity, several thousand years' worth of valuable oral traditions. It is on that basis, that I compiled the earlier volumes of the rational bible series: "What's Wrong with Religion?" and "New Testament Parallels to the Sacred and Secular" which identify the Bible's most likely 1st century editors as well as their sources.

13

Fundamentalist deem, as the word of God, the political babblings of primeval Man having fashioned God in his own flawed image. As a result, the Bible is chocked full of superstitious notions devoid of spiritual value. Yet, as a living document (having drawn on the contributions of some of history's most influential minds), the Bible is also the evolutionary culmination of several thousand years' worth of philosophical thought (See, rationalbible.com). Among them is Jesus, whose life stands as a testament to the value and authenticity of his teachings. In order to grasp the full significance of those truths however, we must realize that even our most beloved personifications of God are inadequate.

"Lest ye corrupt yourselves, and make you a graven image, the similitude of any figure, the likeness of male or female"

–Deuteronomy 4:16

"Confounded be all they that serve graven images, that boast themselves of idols: worship him, all ye gods."

–Psalms 97:7

"They shall be turned back, they shall be greatly ashamed, that trust in graven images, that say to the molten images, Ye are our gods"

–Isaiah 42:17

"They that make a graven image are all of them vanity; and their delectable things shall not profit; and they are their own witnesses; they see not, nor know; that they may be ashamed."

–Isaiah 44:9

"Who hath formed a god, or molten a graven image that is profitable for nothing?"

–Isaiah 44:10

"And the residue thereof he maketh a god, even his graven image: he falleth down unto it, and worshippeth it, and

prayeth unto it, and saith,
Deliver me; for thou art my
god."

–Isaiah 44:17

"Assemble yourselves and
come; draw near together, ye
that are escaped of the nations:
they have no knowledge that
set up the wood of their graven
image, and pray unto a god
that cannot save."

–Isaiah 45:20

"I have even from the
beginning declared it to thee;
before it came to pass I shewed
it thee: lest thou shouldest say,
Mine idol hath done them, and
my graven image, and my
molten image, hath
commanded them."

–Isaiah 48:5

"Every man is brutish in his
knowledge; every founder is
confounded by the graven
image: for his molten image is
falsehood, and there is no
breath in them."

– Jeremiah 10:14 & 51:17

Thy graven images also will I
cut off, and thy standing
images out of the midst of thee;
and thou shalt no more
worship the work of thine
hands.

–Micah 5:13

What profiteth the graven
image that the maker thereof
hath graven it; the molten
image, and a teacher of lies,
that the maker of his work
trusteth therein, to make dumb
idols?

–Habakkuk 2:18

Contrary to fundamentalist belief, being nonreligious does not render one an "a/theist" (one who refutes theism vs. one who refutes the existence of a supernatural being altogether). It requires an equally superstitious and trivial mind either to confirm or deny the existence of a supernatural. It is out of my very love and appreciation for God (truth) in fact, that I prefer reason to that which requires indemonstrable proofs. That is, I seek godliness for its own sake while noting intimate serendipities along the way that seem only to say, "I am here."

15

One inescapable certainty to this life is its inequitable disposition. It is, as they say a "dog-eat-dog" world. And for most of us, no other possibility is conceivable. But Jesus described something altogether different, a place where all people love without regard for race, creed or anything else that separates one from another. He made analogies, referencing the beloved scriptures of his people. While continually repeating the phrase, "the Kingdom of Heaven is like..." Jesus described their promised land as well as the virtues one would have to nurture to reach it. But these truth had been in their hearts all along...

"And forgive thy people that have sinned against thee, and all their transgressions wherein they have transgressed against thee, and give them compassion before them who carried them captive, that they may have compassion on them"   –1 Kings 8:50

"For if ye turn again unto the LORD, your brethren and your children shall find compassion before them that lead them captive, so that they shall come again into this land: for the LORD your God is gracious and merciful, and will not turn away his face from you, if ye return unto him. "   –2 Chronicles 30:9

Albert Einstein once noted that our limited understanding of the Universe is a result of our concept of self, thoughts and feelings as something separated from the whole. He referred to this phenomenon as an "optical delusion" of consciousness. This delusion wrote Einstein, is a kind of prison which restricts affections for a few persons that are nearest to us. Einstein said that the only way for mankind to free themselves from this prison of limited perception is to broaden their "circle of compassion to embrace all living creatures and the whole of nature in its beauty."

Our minds are so consumed by the concerns of this monetized purgatory that we miss the full spectrum and far reaching implications of Jesus' teachings on compassion and goodwill. Many of his parables refer to the forgiveness of debts as an illustration of the "golden rule." The following passage can be found in 18th chapter of Mathew: [23-35]

Jesus: Therefore is the kingdom of heaven likened unto a certain king, which would take account of his servants. And when he had begun to reckon, one was brought unto him, which owed him ten thousand talents. But forasmuch as he had not to pay, his lord commanded him to be sold, and his wife, and children, and all that he had, and payment to be made. The servant therefore fell down, and worshipped him, saying, Lord, have patience with me, and I will pay thee all. Then the lord of that servant was moved with compassion, and loosed him, and forgave him the debt. But the same servant went out, and found one of his fellowservants, which owed him an hundred pence: and he laid hands on him, and took him by the throat, saying, Pay me that thou owest. And his fellowservant fell down at his feet, and besought him, saying, Have patience with me, and I will pay thee all. And he would not: but went and cast him into prison, till he should pay the debt. So when his fellowservants saw what was done, they were very sorry, and came and told unto their lord all that was done. Then his lord, after that he had called him, said unto him, O thou wicked servant, I forgave thee all that debt, because thou desiredst me: Shouldest not thou also have had compassion on thy fellowservant, even as I had pity on thee? And his lord was wroth, and delivered him to the tormentors, till he should pay all that was due unto him. So likewise shall my heavenly Father do also unto you, if ye from your hearts forgive not every one his brother their trespasses.

We cannot be merciful to those whom wield no power over us, but only to those whom we hold dominion over...

"Abstinence is forgiveness only when there is power to punish; it is meaningless when it pretends to proceed from a helpless creature."   –Gandhi

As masters of our own perception, we are judged by the same measure that we hold unto others. Consider the following passage from Matthew 6:9-34:

Jesus: After this manner therefore pray ye: Our Father which art in heaven, Hallowed be thy name. Thy kingdom come. Thy will be done in earth, as it is in heaven. Give us this day our daily bread. And forgive us our debts, as we forgive our debtors. And lead us not into temptation, but deliver us from evil: For thine is the kingdom, and the power, and the glory, for ever. Amen. For if ye forgive men their trespasses, your heavenly Father will also forgive you: But if ye forgive not men their trespasses, neither will your Father forgive your trespasses. Moreover when ye fast, be not, as the hypocrites, of a sad countenance: for they disfigure their faces, that they may appear unto men to fast. Verily I say unto you, They have their reward. But thou, when thou fastest, anoint thine head, and wash thy face; That thou appear not unto men to fast, but unto thy Father which is in secret; and thy Father, which seeth in secret, shall reward thee openly. Lay not up for yourselves treasures upon earth, where moth and rust doth corrupt, and where thieves break through and steal: But lay up for yourselves treasures in heaven, where neither moth nor rust doth corrupt, and where thieves do not break through nor steal: For where your treasure is, there will your heart be also. The light of the body is the eye: if therefore thine eye be single, thy whole body shall be full of light. But if thine eye be evil, thy whole body shall be full of darkness. If therefore the light that is in thee be darkness, how great is that darkness! No man can serve two masters: for either he will hate the one, and love the other; or else he will hold to the one, and despise the other. Ye cannot serve God and mammon. Therefore I say unto you, Take no thought for your life, what ye shall eat, or what ye shall drink; nor yet for your body, what ye shall put on. Is not the life more than meat, and the body than raiment? Behold the fowls of the air: for they sow not, neither do they reap, nor gather into barns; yet your heavenly Father feedeth them. Are ye less than they? Which of you by taking thought can add one cubit unto his stature? And why take ye thought for raiment? Consider the lilies of the field, how they grow; they toil not, neither do they spin: And yet I say unto you, That even Solomon in all his glory was not arrayed like one of these. Wherefore, if God so clothe the grass of the field, which to day is, and to morrow is cast into the oven, shall he not much more clothe you, O ye of little faith? Therefore take no thought, saying, What shall we eat? or, What shall we drink? or, Wherewithal shall we be clothed? (For after all these things do the Gentiles seek;) for your heavenly Father knoweth that ye have need of all these things. But seek ye first the kingdom of God, and his righteousness; and all these things shall be added unto you. Take therefore no thought for the morrow: for the morrow shall take thought for the things of itself. Sufficient unto the day is the evil thereof.

Obviously the preceding passage is a multilayered composite of several evangelistic contributors. But the points are clear (well, almost) and reverberated throughout the Jesus' ministry: Don't betray the will of God for the unjust concerns of this world and do unto others as you would have them do unto you. How can we be both just and unjust at the same time? Moreover, how expect mercy and forgiveness when we ourselves will not give it to those less fortunate or formidable than ourselves?

"All the religions of the world describe God pre-eminently as the Friend of the friendship, Help of the helpless, and Protector of the weak."

–Gandhi

If I were to summarize the theme of the preceding power packed passage it would be: "Hold nothing back! Go all the way!" We should never stifle the voice of truth for fears of material or social loss. Jesus said that we should rejoice when the world rejects us because it's a sign that we are holding the evildoer accountable. Don't think that being vegan will be enough to make a lasting impact. Be a relentless voice for the voiceless. True faith is strengthened by acts of conviction.

"Action for one's own self binds, action for the sake of others delivers from bondage."

-Gandhi

"Do not err, my beloved brethren. Every good gift and every perfect gift is from above, and cometh down from the Father of lights, with whom is no variableness, neither shadow of turning. Of his own will begat he us with the word of truth, that we should be a kind of firstfruits of his creatures. Wherefore, my beloved brethren, let every man be swift to hear, slow to speak, slow to wrath: For the wrath of man worketh not the righteousness of God. Wherefore lay apart all filthiness and superfluity of naughtiness, and receive with meekness the engrafted word, which is able to save your souls. But be ye doers of the word, and not hearers only, deceiving your own selves. For if any be a hearer of the word, and not a doer, he is like unto a man beholding his natural face in a glass: For he beholdeth himself, and goeth his way, and straightway forgetteth what manner of man he was. But whoso looketh into the perfect law of liberty, and continueth therein, he being not a forgetful hearer, but a doer of the work, this man shall be blessed in his deed."

–James 1:16–25

Therefore to him that knoweth to do good, and doeth it not, to him it is sin.

–James 4:17

"If ye know these things, happy are ye if ye do them."

John 13:17

"What is faith worth if it is not translated into action?"

–Gandhi

Remember what Jesus said about building one's philosophical foundation on solid ground? Well, the bedrock of faith is activity...

"Wherefore by their fruits ye shall know them. Not every one that saith unto me, Lord, Lord, shall enter into the kingdom of heaven; but he that doeth the will of my Father which is in heaven. Many will say to me in that day, Lord, Lord, have we not prophesied in thy name? and in thy name have cast out devils? and in thy name done many wonderful works? And then will I profess unto them, I never knew you; depart from me, ye that work iniquity. Therefore whosoever heareth these sayings of mine, and doeth them, I will liken him unto a wise man, which built his house upon a rock: And the rain descended, and the floods came, and the winds blew, and beat upon that house; and it fell not: for it was founded upon a rock. And every one that heareth these sayings of mine, and doeth them not, shall be likened unto a foolish man, which built his house upon the sand: And the rain descended, and the floods came, and the winds blew, and beat upon that house; and it fell: and great was the fall of it.

–Matthew 7:20-27

Many would be activist hesitate for fear of what people might think. But for those who take offence at the truth, there is no real love lost; only status. If we were true Christians, would we not avoid social status like the plague. A more worthy cause of concern would be the passive assumption of guilt. We'd like to think ourselves better for having been vegan but passivity is not enough. Patrons of murder will likely never awaken from their stupor without peaceful confrontation. There is no middle ground, either one actively opposes injustice or passively assumes the burden of guilt.

"He that hath an ear, let him hear what the Spirit saith unto the churches. And unto the angel of the church of the Laodiceans write; These things saith the Amen, the faithful and true witness, the beginning of the creation of God; I know thy works, that thou art neither cold nor hot. I would thou wert cold or hot. So then because thou art lukewarm, and neither cold nor hot, I will spue thee out of my mouth."

–Revelation 3:13-16

"And if it seem evil unto you to serve the LORD, choose you this day whom ye will serve; whether the gods which your fathers served that were on the other side of the flood, or the gods of the Amorites, in whose land ye dwell: but as for me and my house, we will serve the LORD."

-Joshua 24:15

And Elijah came unto all the people, and said, How long halt ye between two opinions? if the LORD be God, follow him: but if Baal, then follow him. And the people answered him not a word.

1Kings 18:21

As for you, O house of Israel, thus saith the Lord GOD; Go ye, serve ye every one his idols, and hereafter also, if ye will not hearken unto me: but pollute ye my holy name no more with your gifts, and with your idols.

-Ezekiel 20:39

He that is not with me is against me; and he that gathereth not with me scattereth abroad.

-Matthew 12:30

"He that is not with me is against me: and he that gathereth not with me scattereth."

-Luke 11:23

Of course, polite society prefers quite protest over the more confrontational forms of activism because the latter forces the accused to either desist or kill, maim or imprison the protestor. Every person retains goodness no matter their wrongdoings and it's through their conscience that we should appeal. We cannot rely solely on reason from those who would patron or profit from the slaughter of the innocent.

"How can one "If ye were of the world, the world would love his own: but because ye are not of the world, but I have chosen you out of the world, therefore the world hateth you. Remember the word that I said unto you, The servant is not greater than his lord. If they have persecuted me, they will also persecute you; if they have kept my saying, they will keep yours also. But all these things will they do unto you for my name's sake, because they know not him that sent me. If I had not come and spoken unto them, they had not had sin: but now they have no cloke for their sin. He that hateth me hateth my Father also. If I had not done among them the works which none other man did, they had not had sin: but now have they both seen and hated both me and my Father. But this cometh to pass, that the word might be fulfilled that is written in their law, They hated me without a cause. But when the Comforter is come, whom I will send unto you from the Father, even the Spirit of truth, which proceedeth from the Father, he shall testify of me: And ye also shall bear witness, because ye have been with me from the beginning." –John 15:19–27

It is easy to see how anyone who relentlessly stands in opposition to the injustices of this world should out expecting persecution every step of the way. Jesus was not put to death for heresy, but because he challenged and unjust and corrupt system of government. That is, he stirred up the people in order to reestablish God's rein (truth) over a deceitful world. And it was for that reason, not "profaning the Sabbath", that he was put to death. Right, wrong or indifferent, anyone who makes a stand against prejudice should first measure the cost. Matthew 8:18-22; Luke 14:27-33; 9:57-62; John 6:60-65

"And whosoever doth not bear his cross, and come after me, cannot be my disciple. For which of you, intending to build a tower, sitteth not down first, and counteth the cost, whether he have sufficient to finish it? Lest haply, after he hath laid the foundation, and is not able to finish it, all that behold it begin to mock him, Saying, This man began to build, and was not able to finish. Or what king, going to make war against another king, sitteth not down first, and consulteth whether he be able with ten thousand to meet him that cometh against him with twenty thousand? Or else, while the other is yet a great way off, he sendeth an ambassage, and desireth conditions of peace. So likewise, whosoever he be of you that forsaketh not all that he hath, he cannot be my disciple.

Ironically, many people profess to be Christians for the sole sake of social acceptance!

Setting out to become a true Christian then, is no small matter to be taken in haste. Jesus tells us first, to sit down and weigh the cost, one that could very well be life as they know it. In this way, the cross becomes a symbol of the martyr. A person such as this is a force (for good) to be reckoned. He or she does not rely on brute "strength," but the relinquishment of it. They speak to the truth without concern for personal or social repercussions for they have weighed the cost in advance. Even the possibility of an afterlife is of no consequence to the martyr who refuses to thrive while others suffer (individualistic heaven/hell paradigm).

Counting the Cost of Inaction

There are no bystanders to social injustice. The witness has but one of two choices: stand in peaceable opposition; or assume fault by association. Anyone who's fallen victim to a hate crime (a bullied child, rape or lynch victim, social segregation, etc.) in the presence of others, can testify to the dehumanizing pain is multiplied by the number of witnesses who fail to act. This is not an isolated phenomenon but an understated norm of "polite" society." There's a steep price for fitting in or thriving in an individualistic society. For one to become richer, another must become poorer. Beauty itself exists in contrasting degree to the sufferings of those less in vogue. Such illusory treasures are of no value in the Kingdom.

The Heart of a Martyr & of a Saint

Ever wondered why so many people, having reached the pinnacle of fortune and fame inevitably die by their own hand? Most people spend their entire lives in chase of a pot of gold at the end of a never ending rainbow. But those few who manage to reach the heights of material success know better.

The inequitable aims of this world cast a long shadow of emptiness and despair. No longer disillusioned, these tragic elite soon realize the worthlessness of what Jesus referred to as "mammon." The disparate heart longs for inequality, thus its misguided and absurd notions of an afterlife as biased as that which is preached in commercialist churches. What sinister paradise shirks the remembrance of a lost loved one suffering eternal damnation? For the very mention of "heaven" conjures especially gruesome images of hell for those who truly "love their neighbors as themselves."

Those who strive for the illusory treasures of this world would be bored to tears in such a netherworld haven where everyone is equally attractive, intelligent and enjoys equal access to unlimited resources. Jesus said, "Except a man be born again, he cannot see the Kingdom of God." John 3:3 Spiritual "rebirth" naturally implies both a relinquishment, or "laying down" of such longings of the flesh and an acceptance, or "taking up" of the urgings of the spirit.

Martyrdom does not imply sacrifice for the true Christian grows to loathe the disparity so prevalent to this world, even to the point that they would welcome death. It is on the verge of awakening (dark night of the soul) in fact, that many of the world's most gifted light bearers (having come to the right conclusion from the wrong perspective) have been lost to suicide. It is of no concern for self however, that the truly enlightened sustains his or her own life, but for the sake of others. The ultimate path of the Christian in developing the heart of the martyr as well as the saint then, is through servantdom.

"Whosoever therefore shall humble himself as this little child, the same is greatest in the kingdom of heaven."
–Matthew 18:4

"And whosoever will be chief among you, let him be your servant."
–Matthew 20:27

"But he that is greatest among you shall be your servant. And whosoever shall exalt himself shall be abased; and he that shall humble himself shall be exalted."
–Matthew 23:11–12

And he sat down, and called the twelve, and saith unto them, If any man desire to be first, the same shall be last of all, and servant of all.
–Mark 9:35

The life of a martyr cannot be taken by force, for it is given freely. Those who seek truth and love above all else, soon realize that the unjust conditions of accepting the treasures of this world imply suffering for another. But I do not believe that people called to waste their lives on fruitless forms of worship. This is the norm for commercialized religions which are propelled by superstitious fears of heaven and hell. The absurd notion of separate souls is a byproduct of the individualistic Western world. But the martyr can serve no greater cause than to defy the lies of oppression. The New testament records more than one occasion where Jesus could have repudiated the testimonies of the false witness that were brought against him, yet he said nothing. (After "counting the costs" in the wilderness, he had already relinquished all ties to his mortal life before his ministry even began.) To squander one's life, does nothing for the innocents who remain to suffer at the hands of evil doers. But the notion of dying or being put to death for refusing to submit to the unjust conditions of this world, symbolizes for me, the perfection of the cross. As of yet, I am unworthy. Yet I know of no greater legacy, than to defy the injustices of animal husbandry.

"So that my soul chooseth strangling, and death rather than my life. I loathe it; I would not live alway; let me alone; for my days are vanity."

–Job 7:15–16

"I said in mine heart, Go to now, I will prove thee with mirth, therefore enjoy pleasure: and, behold, this also is vanity. I said of laughter, It is mad: and of mirth, What doeth it? I sought in mine heart to give myself unto wine, yet acquainting mine heart with wisdom; and to lay hold on folly, till I might see what was that good for the sons of men, which they should do under the heaven all the days of their life. I made me great works; I builded me houses; I planted me vineyards: I made me gardens and orchards, and I planted trees in them of all kind of fruits: I made me pools of water, to water therewith the wood that bringeth forth trees: I got me servants and maidens, and had servants born in my house; also I had great possessions of great and small cattle above all that were in Jerusalem before me: I gathered me also silver and gold, and the peculiar treasure of kings and of the provinces: I gat me men singers and women singers, and the delights of the sons of men, as musical instruments, and that of all sorts. So I was great, and increased more than all that were before me in Jerusalem: also my wisdom remained with me. And whatsoever mine eyes desired I kept not from them, I withheld not my heart from any joy; for my heart rejoiced in all my labour: and this was my portion of all my labour. Then I looked on all the works that my hands had wrought, and on the labour that I had laboured to do: and, behold, all was vanity and vexation of spirit, and there was no profit under the sun. And I turned myself to behold wisdom, and madness, and folly: for what can the man do that cometh after the king? even that which hath been already done. Then I saw that wisdom excelleth folly, as far as light excelleth darkness. The wise man's eyes are in his head; but the fool walketh in darkness: and I myself perceived also that one event happeneth to them all. Then said I in my heart, As it happeneth to the fool, so it happeneth even to me; and why was I then more wise? Then I said in my heart, that this also is vanity. For there is no remembrance of the wise more than of the fool for ever; seeing that which now is in the days to come shall all be forgotten. And how dieth the wise man? as the fool. Therefore I hated life; because the work that is wrought under the sun is grievous unto me: for all is vanity and vexation of spirit. Yea, I hated all my labour which I had taken under the sun: because I should leave it unto the man that shall be after me. And who knoweth whether he shall be a wise man or a fool? yet shall he have rule over all my labour wherein I have laboured, and wherein I have shewed myself wise under the sun. This is also vanity. Therefore I went about to cause my heart to despair of all the labour which I took under the sun. For there is a man whose labour is in wisdom, and in knowledge, and in equity; yet to a man that hath not laboured therein shall he leave it for his portion. This also is vanity and a great evil. For what hath man of all his labour, and of the vexation of his heart, wherein he hath laboured under the sun?"   –Ecclesiastes 2:1-22

"No man can serve two masters: for either he will hate the one, and love the other; or else he will hold to the one, and despise the other. Ye cannot serve God and mammon."

–Matthew 6:24

"He that findeth his life shall lose it: and he that loseth his life for my sake shall find it."

–Matthew 10:39

"Then Peter took him, and began to rebuke him, saying, Be it far from thee, Lord: this shall not be unto thee. But he turned, and said unto Peter, Get thee behind me, Satan: thou art an offence unto me: for thou savourest not the things that be of God, but those that be of men. Then said Jesus unto his disciples, If any man will come after me, let him deny himself, and take up his cross, and follow me. For whosoever will save his life shall lose it: and whosoever will lose his life for my sake shall find it. For what is a man profited, if he shall gain the whole world, and lose his own soul? or what shall a man give in exchange for his soul?"

–Matthew 16:22-26

"And then shall many be offended, and shall betray one another, and shall hate one another."

-Matthew 24:10

"And when he had called the people unto him with his disciples also, he said unto them, Whosoever will come after me, let him deny himself, and take up his cross, and follow me. For whosoever will save his life shall lose it; but whosoever shall lose his life for my sake and the gospel's, the same shall save it. For what shall it profit a man, if he shall gain the whole world, and lose his own soul? Or what shall a man give in exchange for his soul?"

-Mar 8:34-37

That we should be saved from our enemies, and from the hand of all that hate us;

-Luke 1:71

"Blessed are ye, when men shall hate you, and when they shall separate you from their company, and shall reproach you, and cast out your name as evil, for the Son of man's sake."

-Luke 6:22

"But I say unto you which hear, Love your enemies, do good to them which hate you,"

—Luke 6:27

"If any man come to me, and hate not his father, and mother, and wife, and children, and brethren, and sisters, yea, and his own life also, he cannot be my disciple."

—Luke 14:26

"No servant can serve two masters: for either he will hate the one, and love the other; or else he will hold to the one, and despise the other. Ye cannot serve God and mammon."

—Luke 16:13

"Remember Lot's wife. Whosoever shall seek to save his life shall lose it; and whosoever shall lose his life shall preserve it."

—Luke 17:32–33

"The world cannot hate you; but me it hateth, because I testify of it, that the works thereof are evil."

–John 7:7

"And Jesus answered them, saying, The hour is come, that the Son of man should be glorified. Verily, verily, I say unto you, Except a corn of wheat fall into the ground and die, it abideth alone: but if it die, it bringeth forth much fruit. He that loveth his life shall lose it; and he that hateth his life in this world shall keep it unto life eternal. If any man serve me, let him follow me; and where I am, there shall also my servant be: if any man serve me, him will my Father honour. Now is my soul troubled; and what shall I say? Father, save me from this hour: but for this cause came I unto this hour."

–John 12:23-27

Introduction

Mohandas Karamchand Gandhi (1869 –1948) is most remembered for his having led not one, but two separate nations of oppressed brethren from the constraints of a militant government without so much as a single act of aggression. His life and teachings have inspired some of history's most effectual activists; the likes of Martin Luther King, Nelson Mandela, Khan Abdul Ghaffar Khan, James Bevel, Steve Biko, Aung San Suu Kyi and James Lawson.

In the initial stages of research, I set out to identify a singular source of Gandhi's unique perspective but soon realized the impossibility of such an endeavor. Obviously, Gandhi was heavily influenced by Hindu scripture. But he dedicated his life to the pursuit of truth, studying ancient and contemporary writings from around the world while drawing significant parallels between them. In his youth, Gandhi was particularly influenced by Plato's Apology and William Salter's Ethical Religion (1889). In early adulthood, he sought the counsel of the Jain. Most notably, was Shrimad Rajchandra; an ascetic monk philosopher who expounded the virtues of service and compassion for all sentient beings.

In later life, Gandhi was heavily influenced by John Ruskin's book, "Unto This Last" (1862) which used Bible parables to criticize industrial capitalism as an unjust economic system and destructive force on the environment. It was Ruskin's book in fact, that first influenced Gandhi's desire to create communities in which all people worked and received equal pay.

Gandhi often referred to the works of Henry David Thoreau, American author of Walden (who himself, was once imprisoned for his refusal to pay taxes in protest of slavery and the Mexican War). In his famous essay "On the Duty of Civil Disobedience," (1849) Thoreau argued that one's moral duty to defy unjust government rests on self-reliance. It was a famous Russian novelist's interpretation of Jesus' Gospel combined with the teachings of "The Bhagavad Gita" however, that ultimately solidified Gandhi's belief in the necessity of peaceful protest.

"It was the New Testament which really awakened me to the rightness and value of Passive Resistance. When I read in the Sermon on the Mount such passages as "Resist not him that is evil" I was simply overjoyed, and found my own opinion confirmed when I least expected it. The Bhagavad Gita deepened the impression and Tolstoy's The Kingdom of God Is Within You gave it a permanent form."

During his lengthy stays, as political prisoner, Gandhi is said to have carried a copy of Leo Tolstoy's "The Kingdom of God Is Within You" (1894). In the final years of Tolstoy's life, the two began a fond exchange of letters. After Tolstoy's death, Gandhi christened a second communal village, "Tolstoy Farm" in commemoration of his beloved mentor's life.

Some of my contemporaries have suggested that this book could have just as aptly been titled, "Tolstoy's Jesus." After all, Gandhi and Tolstoy shared many of the same convictions. Both Tolstoy and Gandhi believed that the key to understanding Jesus' otherwise mystical sayings and ultimate sacrifice could be found in Matthew[5:38-39]: "Ye have heard that it hath been said, an eye for an eye, and a tooth for a tooth: But I say unto you, that ye resist not evil: but whosoever shall smite thee on thy right cheek, turn to him the other also."

Both Gandhi and Tolstoy were wed with children. Each eventually resolved to lives of chastity. Each relinquished extravagant lifestyles, believing that the private holdings of wealth and property ultimately lead to the oppression of the working classes. An important distinction between Gandhi and Tolstoy however lie, in their interpretation of Jesus' philosophy on nonresistance. Tolstoy's literal interpretation, (also known as "Christian Anarchy") requires total noncooperation with unjust government entities. This relatively passive stance didn't sit well with Gandhi, a lawyer and political giant who believed it one's moral duty to act, rather than to simply observe (Thoreau's influence). For Gandhi, the opposite of love is not hate, but indifference. Like Tolstoy, Gandhi would refuse to defend his own life at the harm, even of an adversarial assailant. But to stand idly by as one entity inflicts harm upon another was for Gandhi, an especially grievous sin. It is under the contention that Gandhi's life are a testament to Jesus' teachings of non-violent opposition, that this book is based. It is only through *loving* _acts_, indicative of compassionate understanding, that one extinguishes the fires of enmity.

This introduction was initially in the form of a "brief" timeline of Gandhi's life. The purpose was to identify the people and events that shaped the young timid boy Mohandas Gandhi into the Mahatma, or "Great Soul." Some 30 pages into the project however, I realized that Gandhi's influences spanned the globe. Just as important as the people and life altering events, was Gandhi's philosophy of Satyagraha (insistence on truth) which was forged by a peaceful blitzkrieg of activist engagements too numerous to list. Gandhi actively planted the seeds of Jesus' ideals from which came the likes of James Bevel, Martin Luther King Jr., and Nelson Mandela. Gandhi's strategy of peaceful protest continues to prove effective in innumerable civil rights movements across the world.

One can't help but wonder where Gandhi found the courage and power of will to do devote endless hours to a cause that would inevitably cost his mortal life? Imagine a loved one taken into bondage or held captive by a foreign oppressor. What bounds would you not cross to free them from such a sinister, perverted or murderous master? Depending on your capacity to love, you'd stop at nothing; not even at the cost of your own life! Only by such depth of love can a Man himself, be free from the tyranny of fear and trepidation. Gandhi developed this depth of love for his people as did Jesus for all mankind. It was in fact, Jesus' testimony that initially fortified Gandhi's belief in nonviolent activism. From that point on, there was no venue to sacred or intimidating to stifle the voice of truth within him. What ideal or philosophical insight could stir a man's soul so deeply that he would trade not only his every possession but his very life for it?

Jesus repeatedly stated that despite what the hypocrites teach, Heaven is not some place in the far off distant sky. He spoke in parables that seemed to illustrate a proverbial veil of perverse darkness cast over the earth. He said that those regarded highest in this world are last in the Kingdom. Like the illusive remains of Eden however, Heaven is in our very midst.

"And saying, Repent ye: for the kingdom of heaven is at hand."

–Matthew 3:2

"From that time Jesus began to preach, and to say, Repent: for the kingdom of heaven is at hand."

–Matthew 4:17

"Blessed are the poor in spirit: for theirs is the kingdom of heaven...   –Matthew 5:3

...Blessed are they which are persecuted for righteousness' sake: for theirs is the kingdom of heaven...   –Matthew 5:10

...Rejoice, and be exceeding glad: for great is your reward in heaven: for so persecuted they the prophets which were before you...

–Matthew 5:12

…Let your light so shine before men, that they may see your good works, and glorify your Father which is in heaven."

–Matthew 5:16

"Take heed that ye do not your alms before men, to be seen of them: otherwise ye have no reward of your Father which is in heaven…

–Matthew 6:1

…Thy kingdom come. Thy will be done in earth, as it is in heaven."

–Matthew 6:10

"And as ye go, preach, saying, The kingdom of heaven is at hand."

–Matthew 10:7

"Another parable put he forth unto them, saying, The kingdom of heaven is likened unto a man which sowed good seed in his field"

–Matthew 13:24

"Another parable put he forth unto them, saying, The kingdom of heaven is like to a grain of mustard seed, which a man took, and sowed in his field"

-Matthew 13:31

"Another parable spake he unto them; The kingdom of heaven is like unto leaven, which a woman took, and hid in three measures of meal, till the whole was leavened...

-Matthew 13:33

...Then said he unto them, Therefore every scribe which is instructed unto the kingdom of heaven is like unto a man that is an householder, which bringeth forth out of his treasure things new and old."

-Matthew 13:52

"And Jesus answered and said unto him, Blessed art thou, Simon Barjona: for flesh and blood hath not revealed it unto thee, but my Father which is in heaven."

-Matthew 16:17

"At the same time came the disciples unto Jesus, saying, Who is the greatest in the kingdom of heaven?...

-Matthew 18:1

…Whosoever therefore shall humble himself as this little child, the same is greatest in the kingdom of heaven."

-Matthew 18:4

"Again I say unto you, That if two of you shall agree on earth as touching anything that they shall ask, it shall be done for them of my Father which is in heaven…

-Matthew 18:19

…Therefore is the kingdom of heaven likened unto a certain king, which would take account of his servants…

-Matthew 18:23

…Then his lord, after that he had called him, said unto him, O thou wicked servant, I forgave thee all that debt, because thou desiredst me: Shouldest not thou also have had compassion on thy fellowservant, even as I had pity on thee? And his lord was wroth, and delivered him to the tormentors, till he should pay all that was due unto him. So likewise shall my heavenly Father do also unto you, if ye from your hearts forgive not every one his brother their trespasses."

-Matthew 18:32-35

"But Jesus said, Suffer little children, and forbid them not, to come unto me: for of such is the kingdom of heaven."

-Matthew 19:14

"For the kingdom of heaven is like unto a man that is an householder, which went out early in the morning to hire labourers into his vineyard."

-Matthew 20:1

"The kingdom of heaven is like unto a certain king, which made a marriage for his son, And sent forth his servants to call them that were bidden to the wedding: and they would not come…"

-Matthew 22:2-3

…Then saith he to his servants, The wedding is ready, but they which were bidden were not worthy. Go ye therefore into the highways, and as many as ye shall find, bid to the marriage."

-Matthew 22:8-9

"For the kingdom of heaven is as a man travelling into a far country, who called his own servants, and delivered unto them his goods…

-Matthew 25:14

...His lord said unto him, Well done, thou good and faithful servant: thou hast been faithful over a few things, I will make thee ruler over many things: enter thou into the joy of thy lord."

-Matthew 25:21

"And when ye stand praying, forgive, if ye have ought against any: that your Father also which is in heaven may forgive you your trespasses...

-Mark 11:25

...But if ye do not forgive, neither will your Father which is in heaven forgive your trespasses."

-Mark 11:26

"And it came to pass, as the angels were gone away from them into heaven, the shepherds said one to another, Let us now go even unto Bethlehem, and see this thing which is come to pass, which the Lord hath made known unto us."

-Luke 2:15

"Rejoice ye in that day, and leap for joy: for, behold, your reward is great in heaven: for in the like manner did their fathers unto the prophets."

–Luke 6:23

"He that cometh from above is above all: he that is of the earth is earthly, and speaketh of the earth: he that cometh from heaven is above all...

–John 3:31

...Our fathers did eat manna in the desert; as it is written, He gave them bread from heaven to eat...

–John 6:31

...For the bread of God is he which cometh down from heaven, and giveth life unto the world...

–John 6:33

...And they said, Is not this Jesus, the son of Joseph, whose father and mother we know? how is it then that he saith, I came down from heaven?...

–John 6:42

…This is the bread which cometh down from heaven, that a man may eat thereof, and not die…

-John 6:50

..I am the living bread which came down from heaven: if any man eat of this bread, he shall live forever: and the bread that I will give is my flesh, which I will give for the life of the world…

-John 6:51

…This is that bread which came down from heaven: not as your fathers did eat manna, and are dead: he that eateth of this bread shall live for ever."

-John 6:58

"But many that are first shall be last; and the last shall be first."

-Matthew 19:30

This is how it was with Gandhi. No earthly power was greater than Gandhi's love for his people. There was no cost too great, nor any venue so sacred as to cause him hesitation.

"I am absolutely convinced that no wealth in the world can help humanity forward, even in the hands of the most devoted worker in this cause. The example of great and pure personages is the only thing that can lead us to find ideas and noble deeds. Money only appeals to selfishness and always irresistibly tempts its owner to abuse it. Can anyone imagine Moses, Jesus or Gandhi with the moneybags of Carnegie?"

–Albert Einstein

As a young law student, Gandhi was for a time, embraced and educated by the elitist oppressors of his people. Reminiscent of the story of Moses, he took lessons in British etiquette, wore expensive "brand name" clothes and for a few months, even gave up vegetarianism. But his parents had sown the seeds of the Kingdom in his heart. Gandhi's first recorded act of non-participative protest was in response to increasingly prejudiced statutes against Indians. Rather than to remove his sacred turban, as other lawyers had done, Gandhi calmly got up and walked out of the courtroom.

From then on, Gandhi's message was akin to Moses' "set my people free!" Those present when Gandhi first turned and walked out of the courtroom, must have said, "What a troublemaker" or "oh, he's one of them." It often seems to be the least "likely to succeed" that are called to the task. But those who answer the call, must prepare to give their all. For there is no greater wealth than a life filled with meaning and purpose.

"Do not worry in the least about yourself, leave all worry to God," this appears to be the commandment in all religions.

-Gandhi

"He answered and said unto them, Because it is given unto you to know the mysteries of the kingdom of heaven, but to them it is not given. For whosoever hath, to him shall be given, and he shall have more abundance: but whosoever hath not, from him shall be taken away even that he hath."

– Matthew 13,11-12

"So when even was come, the lord of the vineyard saith unto his steward, Call the labourers, and give them their hire, beginning from the last unto the first."

–Matthew 20:8

"So the last shall be first, and the first last: for many be called, but few chosen."

–Matthew 20:16

For unto every one that hath shall be given, and he shall have abundance: but from him that hath not shall be taken away even that which he hath.

–Matthew 25:29

And he sat down, and called the twelve, and saith unto them, If any man desire to be first, the same shall be last of all, and servant of all.   –Mark 9:35

But many that are first shall be last; and the last first.

–Mark 10:31

And, behold, there are last which shall be first, and there are first which shall be last.

–Luke 13:30

"And he said unto them, Unto you it is given to know the mystery of the kingdom of God: but unto them that are without, all these things are done in parables: That seeing they may see, and not perceive; and hearing they may hear, and not understand; lest at any time they should be converted, and their sins should be forgiven them. And he said unto them, Know ye not this parable? and how then will ye know all parables? The sower soweth the word. And these are they by the way side, where the word is sown; but when they have heard, Satan cometh immediately, and taketh away the word that was sown in their hearts. And these are they likewise which are sown on stony ground; who, when they have heard the word, immediately receive it with gladness; And have no root in themselves, and so endure but for a time: afterward, when affliction or persecution ariseth for the word's sake, immediately they are offended. And these are they which are sown among thorns; such as hear the word, And the cares of this world, and the deceitfulness of riches, and the lusts of other things entering in, choke the word, and it becometh unfruitful. And these are they which are sown on good ground; such as hear the word, and receive it, and bring forth fruit, some thirtyfold, some sixty, and some an hundred. And he said unto them, Is a candle brought to be put under a bushel, or under a bed? and not to be set on a candlestick? For there is nothing hid, which shall not be manifested; neither was any thing kept secret, but that it should come abroad. If any man have ears to hear, let him hear. And he said unto them, Take heed what ye hear: with what measure ye mete, it shall be measured to you: and unto you that hear shall more be given. For he that hath, to him shall be given: and he that hath not, from him shall be taken even that which he hath. And he said, So is the kingdom of God, as if a man should cast seed into the ground; And should sleep, and rise night and day, and the seed should spring and grow up, he knoweth not how. For the earth bringeth forth fruit of herself; first the blade, then the ear, after that the full corn in the ear. But when the fruit is brought forth, immediately he putteth in the sickle, because the harvest is come. And he said, Whereunto shall we liken the kingdom of God? or with what comparison shall we compare it? It is like a grain of mustard seed, which, when it is sown in the earth, is less than all the seeds that be in the earth. But when it is sown, it groweth up, and becometh greater than all herbs, and shooteth out great branches; so that the fowls of the air may lodge under the shadow of it."

–Mark 4.11–32

Then shall the righteous shine forth as the sun in the kingdom of their Father. Who hath ears to hear, let him hear. Again, the kingdom of heaven is like unto treasure hid in a field; the which when a man hath found, he hideth, and for joy thereof goeth and selleth all that he hath, and buyeth that field. Again, the kingdom of heaven is like unto a merchant man, seeking goodly pearls. Who, when he had found one pearl of great price, went and sold all that he had, and bought it. Again, the kingdom of heaven is like unto a net, that was cast into the sea, and gathered of every kind. Which, when it was full, they drew to shore, and sat down, and gathered the good into vessels, but cast the bad away.

–Matthew 13.43–48

"Live as if you were to die tomorrow. Learn as if you were to live forever."

56

"The greatness of humanity is not in being human, but in being humane." "In a gentle way, you can shake the world." "Change yourself – you are in control." "I will not let anyone walk through my mind with their dirty feet." *"The weak can never forgive. Forgiveness is the attribute of the strong."* "Freedom is not worth having if it does not include the freedom to make mistakes." "We need not wait to see what others do." "A 'No' uttered from the deepest conviction is better than a 'Yes' merely uttered to please, or worse, to avoid trouble." *"To call woman the weaker sex is a libel: it is man's injustice to woman."* "Earth provides enough ~~to satisfy~~ 'Live as if you w~~ere~~ **"The greatness of humanity is not in being human, but in being humane."** "In a gentle way, you can shake the world." "Change yourself – you are in control." "I will not let anyone walk through my mind with their dirty feet." *"The weak can never forgive. Forgiveness is the attribute of the strong."* "Freedom is not worth having if it does not include the freedom to make mistakes." "We need not wait to see what others do." "A 'No' uttered from the deepest conviction is better than a 'Yes' merely uttered to please, or worse, to avoid trouble." *"To call woman the weaker sex is a libel: it is man's injustice to woman."* "Earth provides enough to satisfy every man's needs, but not every man's greed." "Live as if you were to die tomorrow. Learn as if you were to live forever." **"The greatness of humanity is not in being human, but in being humane."** "In a gentle way, you can shake the world." "Change yourself – you are in control." "I will not let anyone walk through my mind with their dirty

Staying the Storm

Jesus arrived at the temple courts in Jerusalem just in time for the Festival of Dedication. He and his disciples sought shelter from the bitter cold at Solomon's Porch where event officials had lie in wait...

Chief Officials: How long will you make us wonder about you? Always showing up in our assemblies; stirring up the people with your strange interpretation of the Law. How dare you teach as if you have authority over the Word of God? If you claim to be Messiah, then come right out and say so!

Jesus: I have answered your questions openly, but you will not acknowledge the authority for which I speak. Even for my works, you will not believe. You will not accept me or my message, because we are not of my flock. My people know me for the things I stand for and I account for them. And because of that, they walk with me. Did the prophet not speak that in every generation...

"I will place shepherds over them who will tend them, and they will no longer be afraid nor will any be missing," declares the LORD."

-JEREMIAH 23:4

Jesus continues: There is none greater than my Father who has entrusted them to me. And since no one is able to snatch them out of my father's hand, neither will they be taken from mine.

By this time, Jesus' fame had spread throughout the land but his popularity was sorely waning. On several occasions, religious extremist gathered stones intending to put Jesus to death on account of heresy ...

Jesus: I assure you that I teach nothing new. My interpretation of the Law as I teach it was revealed to me by the eternal Spirit. And I have done nothing that I have not been led to do. Tell me exactly, what are my offences? Tell me in what manner I have harmed you that I may make amends?

Religionists: We do not condemn you for offenses done toward us. The things you say are an abomination to God!

Another voice from the assembling throng of angry religionists yelled out, "You are but a mortal man, but for your teachings to be true, you would have to be the same as God! That is why we hold you in contempt!"

Jesus: It is written in the scripture that God said, "You are gods." You believe that the whole of scripture is eternal and true, so why would you accuse me of insulting God by citing it?"

On several occasions, Jesus had been openly accused of being a false prophet, a crime punishable by death...

Religionists: Since only you profess to your interpretations of the Law, your testimony is false.

Jesus: The teachings of the Kingdom would remain true even if I alone where to teach it. With my interpretation, the teachings of our people retain value and purpose. But the way you teach it, the Word is lost to vain and superstitious pageantry.

Religionists: Tell us plainly, the nature of this spirit for which you credit your teachings?

Jesus: You say of yourselves that you are the sons of Abraham, and because of that you know the truth. Should you not then, be familiar with the source of his commandments also? If not the Spirit of God, then from whom do you say I receive my teachings?

It is said that Jesus took counsel directly from the "Spirit" on what to say and because of this, the experts could not refute his ministry. Mark 13:11-13; Luke 12:11-12 & 21:14-15 Neither should we, as voices for the voiceless, hesitate to consider the personal repercussions of speaking to the truth.

Jesus: I honor the will of God and because of that, you wish to take my life. Yet you say that "I" am possessed of the Devil. For you, I would give my life freely that you would not commit yourselves to murder. But I ask you sincerely, is it "I" you should condemn?

Religionists: What makes you so special that God would entrust to you, a man not even of the cloth, the same as our father Abraham? Are you greater than he?

Jesus: If I give honor to myself, then the honor is worth nothing. But I do know God! If I were to say otherwise, I would be lying to you. Only by honoring the will of God, do I honor myself. Your father Abraham rejoiced to see the coming of the Kingdom. Should you not do the same?

Officials: What? How can you know anything about what Abraham had seen? You are not even 50 years old!

Jesus: Even before the birth of Abraham was "I am."

As Jesus and his disciples part company with the chief priest, they see a beggar lying by the road just outside the temple area ...

Disciples: Who is at fault that this man cannot fend for himself: He or his parents for not having brought him upright?

Jesus: It is not our purpose to find fault. But to bring light wherever there is darkness.

Jesus spoke to the beggar about the coming of God's Kingdom on earth, a truth so transformative that the townspeople barely recognized him...

Residents: Isn't this the man who always sits and begs?"

Enlightened Man: Yes, it is I who was blind but now can see.

They brought the man to the magistrates to testify against Jesus (rather than for him) because he had ministered on the Sabbath. Never before, had the chief priests and professors of the law seen a person live their whole life without purpose or resolve, only to be made whole in an instant. This once insolent man now stood before them as equals. He spoke with such depth and clarity of understanding that they could find no fault in his doctrine. Rather, they declared publicly that his newfound insights could not be of God, since Jesus had taught him on the Sabbath.

Lawyers: Your newfangled understanding is not of God for you were ministered to on the Sabbath and by a man who is not even ordained by the Church.

The religionists began to wonder secretly amongst themselves about Jesus and the source of his Kingdom teachings however, "Might he truly be of God?"

Lawyers: "Since it was your eyes this man opened, what do you say about him?"

Enlightened Man: He is a prophet.

The professors of the Mosaic Law thought it better to argue that the man had feigned his indolence for the sake of pity. So they sent for his parents…

Lawyers: Is this man your son? You say that he was born without comprehension or respect for the Law. So, how does he stand before us now and argue with such vision and clarity of purpose?"

Parents: This man is indeed our son. And we testify that he was born without regard for the Law of Moses. We do not know how he stands before you now. And we know nothing of this man who opened his eyes. Ask our son, for he is now competent to stand in testimony of himself."

The man's parents answered in this way because the religionist officials had already decreed that anyone who dared profess to Jesus' teachings would be rebuked from the synagogue. To be excommunicated from the church, was considered by many, to be a fate worse than death. The religionist professors of the Law called the once infirm man to stand before them yet again.

Lawyers: It is your charge before God to tell the truth. Admit that this man is no messiah!

Enlightened Man: I cannot say if he is "the messiah." But I do know that I was once blind but now I see.

Lawyers: What did he do to you? Tell us specifically, how did he open your eyes?

Enlightened Man: I have already told you that. But you would not listen to me. Why do you want to hear it again? Do you wish to be one of his disciples too?"

The religionists were humiliated to have been outwitted by a man once deemed heretic; a man whom they considered far beneath themselves. They began to shout offences at him...

Religionists: "You are his follower, not us! We are followers of Moses whom we know was of God. But we know nothing of this man nor the authority for which he speaks!"

Enlightened: I find your confusion truly strange! We are in agreement that God does not talk to sinners, but he will speak to anyone who worships and obeys him. You do not deny that he opened my eyes. Why then, do you wonder where he gets his teachings?

The religionist secretly thought to themselves, "This "Jesus" must be of God. How else could an unlearned man conceive much less convey such truths as these." The church officials excommunicated the man who was once blind despite their personal reservations to the truth...

Lawyers: You were born full of sin and yet you think you can teach us? Get out of our synagogue and stay out!

Hearing that the man had been banished from the church, Jesus sought to reassure him...

Jesus: Remember that the Kingdom teachings are a call to life. The fortunes of the vain; how they wax and they wane. But what is virtuous and true will forever remain.

This newly appointed shepherd asked Jesus how the religionist professors could be so well versed in the law, yet miss for themselves, the significance of the Kingdom teachings...

Jesus: Every plant that my Father in heaven has not planted will be pulled up by the roots. Stay away from the religionists. They profess to lead when they themselves do not know the way. If a blind man leads another blind man, both of them will fall into a ditch.

Hearing this, some religionist officials who had been following Jesus in secret could no longer contain themselves. They made their presence known....

Religionists: What? How can you people listen as this man calls your elders "blind" men?

Jesus: If you were simply blind, you would not be found wanting. But by professing to see that which you clearly cannot, (taking on the yolk of a teacher with impure motives) your fault is far more severe. You can be sure that the one who enters not by the door into the sheepfold, but climbs up by some other way, the same is a thief and a robber. But the one to whom the gatekeeper opens is the true shepherd. And when he leads his sheep, he goes before them and calls them out by name; and they know his voice. But they will not follow a strange voice. Rather, they will flee from it.

With this saying, Jesus referenced the prophecies of Old…

"I will surely assemble, O Jacob, all of thee; I will surely gather the remnant of Israel; I will put them together as the sheep of Bozrah, as the flock in the midst of their fold: they shall make great noise by reason of the multitude of men. The breaker is come up before them:

they have broken up, and have passed through the gate,
and are gone out by it: and their king shall pass before
them, and the LORD on the head of them."

-Micah 2:12-13

In this way, Jesus addressed the experts of the Law. Seeing that some of the common folk missed the scriptural reference and were confused...

Jesus: I assure you, that I am a true Shepherd. And all those who came before me, whom you could not follow were but thieves and robbers. Their teachings seem strange and they did not know you. The thief who comes to you as well-heeled clerics intend only to take and destroy life. But I enter in through the narrow gate whereby life is given in abundance. And I walk before you, not as a hired hand who runs at the sight of a wolf. Without a shepherd, the sheep scatter and die. But I, like any good shepherd would gladly lay down my life in exchange for yours. And because I would give my life, I receive it eternal. For nothing that is given freely can be taken by force. This has been revealed to me by the Spirit.

Jesus continues: There are many more which are not of my particular fold. But they too shall hear and be led by the spirit by which I am led and we will become of one fold, and of one shepherd.

Note: Many religionist congregations, even today, claim exclusive rights to righteous salvation. Obviously, such claims are inconsistent with the teachings of Jesus.

"Like the bee gathering honey from the different flowers, the wise person accepts the essence of the different scriptures and sees only the good in all religions"

–Gandhi

"And other sheep I have, which are not of this fold: them also I must bring, and they shall hear my voice; and there shall be one fold, and one shepherd."

– John 10:16

"And not for that nation only, but that also he should gather together in one the children of God that were scattered abroad. "

– John 11:52

In this way, Jesus rekindled the light of the Kingdom within the man who was once blind. But Jesus wanted him to understand the importance of guarding the gift...

Jesus: The kingdom of heaven is like a seed, sown and left to sprout in the hearts of Men. The planter sows over the whole field without concern for which seeds fall into what place. Some seeds fall along the path and the birds come and eat them. Other seeds fall among stones and though they come up, they soon wither for there is little room for their roots to grow. Others fall among wormwood. Ears may form, but the wormwood chokes them out before they have a chance to fill. But the seeds that fall on fertile ground. These will grow and make up for the lost seed. These seedlings bear ears which fill; yielding thirty, sixty, or even a hundredfold.

Note: Jesus said that the Kingdom would not come in the way that most people think. Fundamentalist Christians insist that Jesus will return as a vengeful God (yet somehow unconditionally loving) raining fire down upon the wicked. Such doctrines are remnants of outdated paternalistic myths not the true teachings Jesus.

The spark of the Kingdom remains within the hearts of all people and will become manifest from within those who nurture it.

"Every expression of truth has in it the seeds of propagation, even as the sun cannot hide its light."

—Gandhi

"If the soil is inwardly rich, the seed will swell ind put forth roots, leaves, stalk, and ears that 'ill with grain. In due season, the Kingdom will reveal itself for harvest."

Leo Tolstoy,

The Gospel in Brief

When Jesus finished speaking, his students questioned his preference for allegory for which he stated a two-fold purpose…

Disciples: Why do you speak to the people in parables?

Jesus: It is given unto you to know the mysteries of the kingdom of heaven, but to them it is not. For whosoever hath, to him, more shall be given. And he shall have more in abundance. But whosoever hath not, from him shall be taken away even that which he does have. For those that know the truth but refuse to see it; and hear the truth but do not listen, neither do they understand. In them, the prophecy of Esaias is fulfilled.

"BY HEARING YE SHALL HEAR, AND SHALL NOT UNDERSTAND; AND SEEING YE SHALL SEE, AND SHALL NOT PERCEIVE. FOR THIS PEOPLE'S HEART IS WAXED GROSS, AND THEIR EARS ARE DULL OF HEARING, AND THEIR EYES THEY HAVE CLOSED. LEST AT ANY TIME THEY SHOULD SEE WITH THEIR EYES, AND HEAR WITH THEIR EARS, AND SHOULD UNDERSTAND WITH THEIR HEART, AND SHOULD BE CONVERTED, AND I SHOULD HEAL THEM."

-Isaiah 6:9-10

Jesus continues, But blessed are your eyes for they see 3and your ears, for they hear. For verily I say unto you, that many prophets and righteous men have desired to see those things which you see and have not seen them. And they have longed to hear those things which you hear, and have not heard them. Hear ye therefore the parable of the sower...

"When any one hears the Gospel of the Kingdom but does not understand it, the wicked one will come and snatch up that which was sown in his heart. This is he which received seed by the way side."

"But he that receives the seed into stony places, the same is he that hears the word and receives it with exceeding joy. But trials and tribulations will arise and because the truth has yet to take root, the seedling will fall by the wayside. He also that received seed among the weeds, is one whom has accepted the word in his heart but allowed the shallow concerns of this world to choke it out. He will not bear fruit."

"But seed that is well planted into good ground is likened unto the one who not only hears the word but protects and nourishes it. And because of his pure convicted heart, bears fruit yielding some thirty, sixty, even hundredfold!"

Note: Many who claim to be Christian can recite written scripture backwards and forwards without understanding the nature of the spirit residing within their own hearts. In professing to see the value of the Kingdom however, the commercial religionists inevitably divert what is God's for their own devices. This is the equivalent to propogating the seeds of an unjust world in good soil. Jesus spoke in parables to warn the pretenders of his age, that their deceitfulness is not without consequence. At the same time he reached out to those who truly wished to nourish the seeds of the Kingdom within their own hearts. It is no wonder, that the gospels present Jesus as having rephrased or restated the parable of the sower on multiple occasions.

"I like your Christ.

I do not like your Christians.

Your Christians are so unlike your Christ."

Mahatma Gandhi

In the preceding parable of the sower, Jesus points out that many who initially understand the Gospel and happily receive it, will be robbed of it before they fully accept it into their heart. Their vision is like the seed left exposed by the wayside or choked out among the thorns. The illusory concerns of this realm will come and take it from them. Those who receive the Gospel with hardened hearts represent the seeds that fell on stony ground. They can recite the teachings verbatim, but their joy is superficial. The storm will come and their temples (built on shoddy foundations of sand) will fall. That which is sown among the weeds and the thorns can be likened unto a man who understands the significance of the kingdom, but worldly cares and eagerness for riches strangle the life from him before he bears fruit. To those who search for enlightenment for deceptive purposes or self-aggrandizement, mistakenly plant the seeds of darkness within their own hearts. To them, whatever light they may have had; will be lost. But then there are those who seek enlightenment wholeheartedly for the sake of the Kingdom. To them, more will be given. More important than the means, are the motives underlying one's spiritual endeavors. Gone unchecked, many will barter the good seed for the bad. It is encouraging however, to think that the truth need only take root in the hearts of a few. Under the right conditions, a spark is all that's needed for the Kingdom to sprout like wildfire on earth as it is in heaven.

Then, Jesus gave them another parable...

Jesus: The kingdom of heaven can be likened to a grain of mustard seed, which a man took, and sowed in his field. Now the mustard seed is among the least of all seeds. But when it is nourished, the seed becomes a great tree, so that the birds of the air come and lodge in the branches thereof.

Tolstoy once related a single spark of the Kingdom to an "immaterial speck." When properly tended, it will grow into a magnificent tree befitting the birds of Heaven to nest in it.

Jesus: The Kingdom of Heaven can be likened to what happens when a woman has hidden a little yeast in three measures of meal. Eventually, all the dough will rise.

In the parable of the tares Matthew 13:24-30 Jesus addresses a mixed audience. With astonishingly few words, he addresses the concerns both of the Kingdom within and the Kingdom without; he warns his followers that many who receive sight could be likened to a farmer who, in his slumber received bad seed among the good; even still, he warns the imposters that though placed there by the enemy in secret, their deeds will be brought to light.

Jesus: The Kingdom of Heaven can be likened to a farmer who sowed only good seed in his field. While everyone was sleeping however, the enemy came and scattered tare seeds and left the field undetected. Normally, the servant's would pull the weed, lest it choke out the wheat. But with this particular variety (possibly "bearded darnel" which resembles degenerative wheat) the workers could not distinguish the wheat from the tares. Only after the crop came up and began to ripen did the servants see that much of the "crop" had produced no fruit. The servants came and asked, "Sir, did you not scatter good seed in your field?" An enemy did this," he replied. His servants then asked, "Do you want us to go out and pull up the weeds?" "No!" he answered. "If you do that, you might pull up the good along with the bad. Leave the weeds alone until harvest time. Then I'll tell my reapers to bundle first the tares and burn them but gather the wheat into my barn."

In this way, Jesus warned his followers to keep a watchful eye for the deceitful one's who would plant within their hearts what looked good seed but in the end, would prove to be weeds that only choke out the wheat.

Again and again, Jesus warns the spiritual seeker that though few find the way, many profess to teach it. In the above passage, he simultaneously warns the deceitful that they are wrong to they think their deception goes unnoticed. The reader is however, easily thrown off by the distinctly violent thread of early Roman influence prevalent throughout the conclusion of this parable (as with the cursing of the temple, the fig tree, etc.). Over the course of this book, we'll cover just a few instances where the implication of damnation robs Jesus' teachings of meaning. But there are many more.

Note: Personally, I doubt that Jesus would have threatened damnation to the disbeliever. The spirit of vengeance is an artifact of this "dog-eat-dog" realm, not of the Kingdom he envisioned. Jesus taught his followers to love unconditionally. His life purpose was to usher the coming of God's Kingdom on earth, not to depict a God so vengeful that he would destroy his own "children" with fire! Why then did the Scribes insist on adding such dark and inconsistent undertones? Perhaps, they set out to depict Jesus as having fulfill yet another prophecy of old.

"I WILL OPEN MY MOUTH IN A PARABLE: I WILL UTTER DARK SAYINGS OF OLD: WHICH WE HAVE HEARD AND KNOWN, AND OUR FATHERS HAVE TOLD US."

-PSALMS 78:2-3

The authors of Matthew [13:34] and Mark [4:34] even go so far as to say that every word Jesus spoke was a parable (a double narrative utilizing commonly understood themes to convey a moral). We can find the phrase "dark sayings" throughout the Old Testament prophesies.

"To know wisdom and instruction; to perceive the words of understanding; To receive the instruction of wisdom, justice, and judgment, and equity; To give subtlety to the simple, to the young man knowledge and discretion. A wise man will hear, and will increase learning; and a man of understanding shall attain unto wise counsels: To understand a proverb, and the interpretation; the words of the wise, and their dark sayings."

–Proverbs 1:2–6

An interesting marker of what appears to be among the more authentic sayings originally attributed to Jesus is that they address everyone within earshot. But the beauty of this phenomenon is missed for the constant bombardment with fire and brimstone references. The scribes obviously attributed a negative connation to the term "dark sayings." Interestingly however, the International Standard Bible Encyclopedia renders it (חידות, hīdhoth or hīdhah) to signify simply a "riddle" or "proverb".

The threat of eternal fire and damnation is absent in what was probably among Jesus' most favored Jewish passages which conveys the futility of preserving a superficial legacy. To have lived without a greater purpose is to have never existed at all.

"My mouth shall speak of wisdom; and the meditation of my heart shall be of understanding. I will incline mine ear to a parable: I will open my dark saying upon the harp. Wherefore should I fear in the days of evil, when the iniquity of my heels shall compass me about? They that trust in their wealth, and boast themselves in the multitude of their riches; None of them can by any means redeem his brother, nor give to God a ransom for him: (For the redemption of their soul is precious, and it ceaseth for ever.) That he should still live for ever, and not see corruption. For he seeth that wise men die, likewise the fool and the brutish person perish, and leave their wealth to others. Their inward thought is, that their houses shall continue for ever, and their dwelling places to all generations; they call their lands after their own names. Nevertheless man being in honour abideth not: he is like the beasts that perish. This their way is their folly: yet their posterity approve their sayings. Selah. Like sheep they are laid in the grave; death shall feed on them; and the upright shall have dominion over them in the morning; and their beauty shall consume in the grave from their dwelling. But God will redeem my soul from the power of the grave: for he shall receive me. Selah. Be not thou afraid when one is made rich, when the glory of his house is increased; For when he dieth he shall carry nothing away: his glory shall not descend after him. Though while he lived he blessed his soul: and men will praise thee, when thou doest well to thyself. He shall go to the generation of his fathers; they shall never see light. Man that is in honour, and understandeth not, is like the beasts that perish."

-Psalms 49:3-20

What greater hell than a frivolous life?

The religionist's depiction of heaven and hell, is as absurd and dated as the notion of voodoo for spiritual enlightenment. No just and loving "Father" would damn his own children to an eternal lake of fire. What worthwhile lesson can be learned from such an atrocious and retrograde form of discipline? No less, one that lasts for all eternity with no further chance of parole. Fire and brimstone references might seem forthcoming to the scribe who failed to see for himself, the value of a purpose-filled life. Corporal punishment however, is the antithesis of Jesus' core teachings on compassion and nonresistance to evil. Perhaps, these inconsistent references are among the weeds that Jesus warned about in the parable of the tares (see pgs. 75-76). The spirit of deceit is enemy who planted weeds among the wheat to rob the garden of what is good.

The mere thought of a loved one being eternally damned transforms the nirvana of heaven into the very pits of hell. And as for the irrational premises of separable hereafters; no one would pain more deeply for the potentially condemned than the embodiment of love.[1 John 4:8, 12-13 & 16] Jesus' intended message was that Heaven is not some far off place in the distant future. The Kingdom of God is at hand. [Deu 15:9; Mat 3:2; 4:17; 10:7; 26:45-46; Mark 1:15; 14:42; Rom 13:12; 2Th 2:2; 2Ti 4:6; 1Pe 4:7]

Jesus: The Kingdom of God will not come as most men think. So, if any man should say to you, "See, it is here!" or "over there!" Do not be misled, for the kingdom of God is among you. Because there will be false Christ's and false prophets, and they will give signs and wonders in the hope of turning even the saints from the true way.

The Kingdom of Heaven is well within our grasp. But its fulfillment requires that we be slow to offend or take offence. All around us are the fruits of the good seed along with the thorns of despair. But we miss that when our hearts become susceptible to infraction. The relentless pursuit of truth is as a guerilla at the gate. Without it, the "enemy" will come and plant the seeds of deceit (complacency, fear, doubt, etc.) and we fall back into slumber.

Like never before, we have the means to realize Jesus' Kingdom vision on a global level. Yet, because we do not heed his warnings on an individually; we fall victim to the unyielding temptations of this technological Age. We expect to find portrayals of sex and violence the moment we log onto the internet or tune into our favorite TV or radio "program." These negative coping mechanisms are the root cause of our collective misery. Because we don't allow the seeds of the truth to take root, we fall prey to the temptations of this perpetual cycle of deceit.

The parable of the tares is one of many instances where the New Testament records Jesus as having warned both the sincere follower and the hypocrite simultaneously. Jesus continually warned his followers that there were wolves among them. But in the end, even the darkest of deeds will be brought to light. One compelling notion (blotted out by extraneous references to fire and brimstone) is that the workings of inequity, at least for now, are part of a grand design. In the following parable, notice how the dual meaning of Jesus' message is canceled out by the conclusory threat of damnation followed by a repetition of statements.

Jesus: Because strait is the gate, and narrow is the way, which leads unto life, and few there be that find it, you should be weary of false prophets. They come to you in sheep's clothing, but inwardly they are ravening wolves. **Ye shall know them by their fruits.** Do men gather grapes of thorns, or figs of thistles? Even so every good tree brings forth good fruit; but a corrupt tree brings forth evil fruit. But a good tree cannot bring forth evil fruit, no more than a corrupt tree can bring forth good fruit. ~~Every tree that does not bring forth good fruit is hewn down, and cast into the fire.~~ Wherefore by their fruits ye shall know them.

Throughout this book, we'll discuss innumerable references to the Old Testament imbedded within the sayings attributed to Jesus. Admittedly, they often correspond more closely to the Septuagint (a flawed Greek translation of Mosaic Law) than the more accurate King James translation. While this further disproves notions of a historically accurate depiction of Jesus, it does not discount the value of myth in preserving the long forgotten yet invaluable philosophies of old.

"Then said he unto them, Therefore every scribe which is instructed unto the kingdom of heaven is like unto a man that is an householder, which bringeth forth out of his treasure things new and old."

–Matthew 13:52

From a very young age, I rejected the irrational philosophies of the Orthodox Church. In my search for meaning, I amassed a relatively large library of contemporary knowledge. Yet, what I eventually found amidst New Testament's sea of anti-Semitism is worth more to me now, than my entire lifetime of beautiful thoughts and personal epiphanies.

"A true Brahmin should be the very image of humility and not be proud of his knowledge or wisdom."

–Gandhi

Jesus never claimed to be the sole embodiment of an omnipotent God. He said that we are all children of God. Moreover using the phrase, "Heaven is like..." Jesus sought to differentiate his teachings from the fantastical "castles in the sky" depictions of false prophets. Jesus' message was simple: we project the external world from within our own hearts. That is our greatest gift!

Jesus. The Kingdom of Heaven is like what happens when someone finds immeasurable treasure hidden in a field and buries it again. This person will happily go and sell everything he owns just to buy that buy that field. The kingdom of heaven is like what happens when a shop keeper goes looking for fine pearls. After finding one of immense value, he goes and sells everything else just to buy that pearl.

In both parables, Jesus describes a situation in which a person is willing to barter a life's worth of treasure for this one thing they've spent their whole lives in search of. That's exactly what Jesus told his disciples to do for the sake of the Kingdom...

"Jesus said unto him, if thou wilt be perfect, go and sell that thou hast, and give to the poor, and thou shalt have and thou shalt have treasure in heaven; and come and follow me.   –Matthew 19.21

"Then Jesus beholding him loved him, and said unto him, One thing thou lackest: go thy way, sell whatsoever thou hast, and give to the poor, and thou shalt have treasure in heaven: and come, take up the cross, and follow me."

–Mark 10:21; Luke 18:22

"Sell that ye have, and give alms; provide yourselves bags which wax not old, a treasure in the heavens that faileth not, where no thief approacheth, neither moth corrupteth.

–Luke 12:33

No wonder his popularity was waning with the well-healed religionists who secured and retained their esteemed positions on the whim of occupying Rome. The doctors of the Law sought to squelch anything that stirred the spirits of their oppressed Jewish counterparts. Because commercial religionists do not internalize the philosophies they profess to teach, they derive no inherent value in their work (which is a means for procuring wealth and status). Rather, they present ancient metaphors as literal fact. It is on account of this, that so many people attend church "religiously" never having heard more than a few select passages from Jesus' Sermon on the Mount. Imagine the paradigm altering effect, should Jesus' full message be preached in every venue worldwide!

How did history's most infamous activist become impervious to social norms? Because he was not recognized by the elders of the church, Jesus was held in contempt. Yet he ministered everywhere he went, even in their Synagogues. When visiting his own hometown, the people expressed disdain that a man of such modest beginnings could appoint himself among the chancellors of the sacred Law. Not only that, he took command over it!

Townsfolk: Isn't he the son of the carpenter? Isn't Mary his mother, and aren't James, Joseph, Juda, and Simon his brothers? Doesn't his sisters continue to live among us? How can he do these things on his own authority?"

Jesus: Prophets are honored by everyone, except the people of their hometown and of their own family.

When we think of great leaders, one characteristic comes to mind: charisma. The most common human trait however, is a desire to be liked by others. It stands to reason then, that likeable people don't necessarily make the best initiators of change.*

*The bad news: you simply can't say the "right" thing to the wrong person. New Testament accounts indicate that some of Jesus' closest relatives refused his teachings. Matthew 12:46-49; Mark 3:31-34; Luke 8:19-21, 14:26

The good news, is that you simply can't say the wrong thing to the right people. Always speak the truth. It's no secret that innocent creatures are being slaughtered for fun and profit and the killing will continue so long as we accept of ourselves, even the lamest excuses for standing idly by. But Jesus vindicated no hesitation from his followers. In fact, he told his would-be-disciples to prepare nothing for their journey. Should they be accepted into a home, they were to stay in that town and minister from there. Whenever rejected, they are not to engage in a battle of wits, but rather to knock the dust of their feet in protest against them. That's the modern day equivalent of shouting, "NEXT!"

"And commanded them that they should take nothing for their journey, save a staff only; no scrip, no bread, no money in their purse. But be shod with sandals; and not put on two coats. And he said unto them, In what place soever ye enter into an house, there abide till ye depart from that place. And whosoever shall not receive you, nor hear you, when ye depart thence, shake off the dust under your feet for a testimony against them…"

–Matthew 10:13; Mark 6:11; Luke 9:5 &10:11

People were divided over the Kingdom teachings wherever Jesus taught. Some would say, "Why listen to the senseless jabbering of a man possessed?" But those who received even a glimpse of the Kingdom said, "A demon closes the eyes of a fool, he does not open them."

The Bible tells us that Jesus considered himself something of a prophet. Some even said of him, "It is Elijah" the greatest prophet of all. King Herod feared that Jesus was John the Baptist (whom he'd recently beheaded) resurrected from the dead. People simply thought that way 2000 years ago. Such absurdity remains surprisingly common even amidst the so called "Age of Reason." Many commercial Christians assert that Jesus is the incarnation of a vengeful God, whom so loved the world that he gave himself (his own only son) as a perfect sacrifice to appease himself of fury over the sins of Man. If you think about it, that makes perfect sense. After all, "He" designed us to not to question such inconsistent drivel, right?

The truth does not rest on a foundation of manipulation. The petty peddlers of fear based faith prey on superstitious minds. How does one present the "working of miracles" (Immaculate Conception, walking on water or turning it into wine, etc.) as LOGICAL proofs of anything? These are the tools of manipulation. True faith is a characteristic of an honest Man, not a magi. If not the God of all creation incarnate, how did Jesus come about his revolutionary teachings anyway? To answer that question, we should rewind to beginning of his ministry...

"Live as if you were to die tomorrow. Learn as if you were to live forever."

"The greatness of humanity is not in being human, but in being humane." "In a gentle way, you can shake the world." "Change yourself – you are in control." "I will not let anyone walk through my mind with their dirty feet." *"The weak can never forgive. Forgiveness is the attribute of the strong."* "Freedom is not worth having if it does not include the freedom to make mistakes." "We need not wait to see what others do." "A 'No' uttered from the deepest conviction is better than a 'Yes' merely uttered to please, or worse, to avoid trouble." *"To call woman the weaker sex is a libel; it is man's injustice to woman."* "Earth provides enough to satis   as if you were to d   e

greatness of humanity is not in being human, but in being humane." "In a gentle way, you can shake the world." "Change yourself – you are in control." "I will not let anyone walk through my mind with their dirty feet." *"The weak can never forgive. Forgiveness is the attribute of the strong."* "Freedom is not worth having if it does not include the freedom to make mistakes." "We need not wait to see what others do." "A 'No' uttered from the deepest conviction is better than a 'Yes' merely uttered to please, or worse, to avoid trouble." *"To call woman the weaker sex is a libel; it is man's injustice to woman."* "Earth provides enough to satisfy every man's needs, but not every man's greed." "Live as if you were to die tomorrow. Learn as if you were to live forever." **"The greatness of humanity is not in being human, but in being humane."** "In a gentle way, you can shake the world." "Change yourself – you are in control." "I will not let anyone walk through my mind with their dirty

One Among You...

John, an austere sage from the wilderness of Judaea, ministered on the importance of single-minded devotion. Unlike orthodox professors of Mosaic Law who dressed in expensive robes and slept in stately palaces, John literally lived off the land. His robe consisted wholly of camel hair belted with a strap. But John offered the people something they had never before seen...

John, Prepare the way for the Lord, make his paths straight. Make straight, what is crooked and make smooth what is rough. Fill every valley and bring low every mountain and hill between you and God.

Note: Some contributors to Mathew[3:3-4], Mark[1:3-6]; and Luke [3:4] depict John as the reincarnation of the Old Testament prophet, Elijah[Isaiah 35:8; 57:14; 62:10-11; Malachi 3:1; 4:5-6]. Presented as pure allegory however, these embellishments along with the above passage serve to remind us of how even the smallest improprieties separate us from the realization of profound truths.

People came from all around to hear John speak. But only one would fully grasp the significance of his teachings. His name of course, was Jesus.

John: I baptize with water but there standeth one among you, whom ye know not;

The Jewish people held nothing more sacred than their beloved Torah which promised them, as "God's chosen few", a warrior messiah who would deliver them from the clutches of their Roman oppressors. Their faith concentrated heavily on an absolute obedience to the church, and its superficial doctrines. To question the teachings of the Torah was a crime punishable by death. John however, welcomed the questions of his followers.

John's disciples: How should we go about clearing a path for God?

John: Let those that have more than one coat give to those who have none, and let them that have food, give to those that are hungry.

Rome levied taxes against the Jews and employed their fellow countrymen to collect. These tax collectors did not receive direct compensation from Rome however. Rather, they were to charge the tax payer (at their discretion) for services rendered. Needless to say, these folks were loathed as traitors. Ostracized as outcasts, no member of polite society would be seen interacting with them.

Unlike the orthodox priests, John welcomed every person equally, rejecting neither the tax collectors nor the occupying Roman soldiers. He advised them simply: "Do not cause harm," and "be content with what is freely offered for your services." At first, John is presented as an austere minister of peace who accepts everyone equally. But when he saw many of the orthodox religionists (Pharisees and Sadducees) coming to be baptized, he flips the script...

John: O generation of vipers, who hath warned you to flee from the wrath to come? Bring forth therefore fruits meet for repentance: And think not to say within yourselves, "We have Abraham to our father: for I say unto you, that God is able to raise up children for Abraham from these very stones." And now also the axe is laid unto the root of the trees: every tree which does not bring forth good fruit will be hewn down, and cast into the fire. I indeed baptize you with water unto repentance: but one is coming after me who is mightier than I, whose shoes I am not worthy to bear: he shall baptize you with the Holy Ghost, and with fire: Whose fan is in his hand, and he will throughly purge his floor, and gather his wheat into the garner; but he will burn up the chaff with unquenchable fire.

Here, the New Testament authors have transformed John the Baptist from an austere minister of peace (who lived off the land and told his followers to sell everything they owned and give to the poor) to a crazed fire and brimstone prophet of doom. Again, the notion of eternal damnation is antithesis Jesus' vision for a world at peace. There is reason to believe however, that John was a member of the Essenes, a Judaic sect that considered themselves to be "children of light." Essene scripture (the Dead Sea Scrolls) foretold of an apocalyptic war that would wipe out the "children of darkness." Why would John call those who came to be baptized by him, *"offspring of poisonous snakes?"* Furthermore, what did he mean by asking, "Oh! *Who warned you* to run from the coming wrath of God?"

The Essenes regarded themselves as "keepers of secrets" including a prophecy which involved a warrior messiah (the one who would bring about the aforementioned apocalypse) that would rise up and lead them to victory. The only other Jewish sects mentioned in the canonical Gospels during the time of Jesus were the Sadducees and Pharisees. The entire 23rd chapter of Matthew is dedicated to Jesus' verbal rebukes to both of these particular sects. So, by the process of elimination alone, we can deduce that John and Jesus were members of the Essene.

"Let your change of heart be seen by your works. Oh, and do not expect favor as the sons of Abraham. God can raise up children for Abraham out of these stones!"

Other than the questionable writings of loathsome "historians" like Flavius Josephus (who probably edited much of the New Testament) and Pliny the Elder (who probably copied verbatim from the works of Josephus) we know very little of the Essenes, Supposing that Josephus based at least some of his fantastical claims on actual people and events, we can further deduce that the Essenes observed rigorous ideals of purity including vegetarianism, celibacy, charity and the relinquishment of personal property. They studied ancient Hebrew scripture, spiritually immersed themselves in water, ate together after prayer and generally forbade the expression of anger. The Essenes rejected the superficial rituals performed by the Sadducees and Pharisees (especially animal sacrifice). Believing that the church was corrupt, they retreated into the wilderness just as Elijah and Moses had done before them. What remains of the Dead Sea Scrolls are pictured below.

The Embodiment of Love

In making sense of the New Testament, we can deduct that Jesus was inspired by John the Baptist. The NT tells us that after being baptized by his famed cousin and mentor, Jesus joined the Essene regimen of fasting and reflecting in the wilderness. It was there that he confronted three concerns of the ego: doubt, pride, and the desire for wealth and status. 40 days later, Jesus would emerge with an intimate understanding of the commandments given to Moses 1400 years earlier. Rather than a "keeper of secrets" however, Jesus openly conveyed the hidden knowledge of the Essenes with anyone who would listen.

"For nothing is hidden except to be made manifest; nor is anything secret except to come to light. If anyone has ears to hear, let him hear."

–Mark 4:22-23

"Nothing is covered up that will not be revealed, or hidden that will not be known. Therefore whatever you have said in the dark shall be heard in the light, and what you have whispered in private rooms shall be proclaimed on the housetops."

–Luke 12:2-3

Jesus' Last Fast

Jesus was led into the wilderness to fast and pray for 40 days and nights just as Moses and Elijah had done before him. He would emerge with a much more exacting form of the commandments than even Moses had received. (Though Jesus' was condensed into five.) After some time fasting in the wilderness, Jesus became hungry and overwhelmed by the spirit of doubt.

The First Temptation

The Spirit of Doubt "If you are a child of God, command that these stones be made bread."

There are times in our spiritual journey when we feel almost invulnerable to our old ways of thinking. But then the spirit of doubt inevitably creeps in as if to say...

"You must NOT ignore the desires of the flesh for the Spirit placed them upon you. It is therefore, the will of God that you attend to them."

Such an argument seems most sound when we are at our weakest. It is the nature of man to rationalize even our most irrational behaviors. But Jesus relied on the scripture for spiritual sustenance.

The Mark of a Christian Leader

What rational purpose might there have been, for Jesus to venture off into the wilderness? Remember that John had already identified him as one among the many who would rise up and separate the "wheat from the chaff." The true leader is the "least" self-serving, most humble member of the group. He or she has, at least for a time, relinquished all concern for their present existence (desiring of material wealth, status etc.) and any other chasm between it and God (the true spiritual or ideal self). After following in the traditions of Moses and Elijah (fasting and praying in solitude for 40 days and nights) Jesus emerged with a condensed version of the 10 commandments.

Contrary to the norm, the goal of Christianity should not be to exalt, but to diminish one's desire for inequity from others. One cannot raise others up by tearing them down, but on by humbling themselves. "To be perfect," as Jesus put it, one must relinquish all ties or concerns of this unjust world in favor of the Kingdom. Your flesh requires nourishment and shelter, but you are more than the sum of its parts. The spirit (love) requires compassion and mercy. As an industrial-organizational psychologist, I can tell you that there is a very compelling reason large corporations continue to pay trillions of dollars in commercial "programing" each year. They want to "capitalize" on that feeling of emptiness that "whole" that only empathy can fill. Unless and until we take the time to "unplug" or separate ourselves from what many people refer to as the "media matrix" we will never be free from its purposely misguided values.

Jesus: "Man shall not live by bread alone, but by every word that proceeds out of the mouth of God."

Most of us walk around with a little cynic in our heads, comparing our every move to the behaviors and apparent status of others. When Jesus encountered this "voice of doubt" in the wilderness, he called on Deuteronomy [8:3] to form a response :

"And he humbled thee, and suffered thee to hunger, and fed thee with manna, which thou knewest not, neither did thy fathers know; that he might make thee know that man doth not live by bread only, but by every word that proceedeth out of the mouth of the LORD doth man live."

In the preceding instance, Jesus drew on Israel's 40 years trek through the wilderness...

"You shall remember all the ways that the Lord your God has led you in the wilderness these forty years, that He might humble you, testing you, to know what was in your heart, whether you would keep His commandments or not. Your clothing did not wear out on you, nor did your feet swell these forty years. "Thus you are to know in your heart that the Lord your God was disciplining you just as a man disciplines his son."

The first temptation of the Israelites after having escaped the clutches of Egypt was also the spirit of doubt. They thought, "At least the Egyptians clothed us and fed us. What good is liberation when it leads to starvation?" In Jesus' case, he might have thought "what good is spiritual liberation if I starve to death in the process." How many times have we started out on a mission only to turn back with our tails between our legs thinking, "If it's this hard... I'd rather... it wasn't that bad after all... at least I had..." Jesus told his followers to sell all material possessions (excepting only the clothes on their back) and give to the poor. Each of us must equally overcome the temptation of doubt before we can truly call ourselves the followers of Jesus and leaders of Men.

The hesitant activist thinks, "I need time to prepare myself for the arduous journey ahead." But when Jesus sent his disciples on a pilgrimage, he forbade them from carrying money or even think of what they will say! He told them rather, to leave all their concerns behind, relying on the Spirit (good of others) for sustenance. Many must have thought, "Wishful thinking, that sounds good and all but it's just not the way the world works. If I give all that I have to others, then who will take care of me?" From a purely rational perspective, that is probably what was going on in Jesus' mind at this juncture of his initiation. But he prevailed because he called on his pool of wisdom or scripture for spiritual sustenance. It is for this reason that I started rationalbible.com where readers can find hundreds of free downloads and other informational and inspirational resources.

The Second Temptation

Jesus told his followers that to come to see the significance of a Kingdom (a world without disparity) they must be poor of heart. This is what it means to be meek; without desire for wealth or status or any other effect of social inequity. Many who endure "dark nights of the soul" have come to realize the illusive treasures of this realm inevitable lead to "despair." Some become bearers of light but others lose their way and squander their insight with incessant diversions (unnatural concentrated foods, drugs, pleasure seeking and concerns of the occult and other forms of slow and steady spiritual suicide).

"For in much wisdom is much grief; and he that increaseth knowledge increaseth sorrow."

–Ecclesisates 1:18

In this way, Jesus was tempted a second time. As he sat on a very high place, Jesus was overwhelmed by the Spirit of Pride.

Spirit of Pride: If you are truly a child of light then throw yourself from this place. For it is written, He shall give His angels charge concerning Thee; and in their hands they shall bear Thee up, lest at any time Thou dash Thy food against a stone.

Note: We know that the Essenes regarded themselves as keepers of secrets, one of which was the names and evocations of Angels. Should Jesus jump from the cliff and die, it would surely put an end to any undesirable longings and existential sufferings which are an otherwise inescapable part of the human condition. Either outcome (death, or the enslavement of "spirits") however, does nothing to advance the Kingdom. Again, Jesus calls on his scripture for physical strength and spiritual sustenance.

Jesus: It is written again, Thou shalt not test the Lord thy God."

Even if Jesus were to jump from a cliff and invoke power over "angels" to safely and miraculously lower himself to the ground, it would most definitely endorse the occult knowledge of the Essenes. But again, mysticism does nothing to advance the Kingdom of Heaven. To squander one's life in search of the arcane is the choice of a prideful fool rather than a humble servant. It makes no difference to a principled life, the existence of some mythical or mystical (real or imagined) realm. The Kingdom of Heaven is in our midst, here and now. Occult practices such as the sham working of miracles have nothing to do with the works of virtue. One's longing for power, one over another, only diminishes the inherent value of a good and moral life.

There is a difference between praying for life on Earth to be "as it is in Heaven", and praying for miracles as proof that God or angels exist. The takeaway message of Jesus' second temptation is: DON'T ASK IN YOUR OWN SUTTLE WAYS FOR GOD TO VALIDATE YOUR FAVOR. Why do the authors of Matthew[4:5-7] have Jesus quoting from Psalm [91] and Deuteronomy [6:16]?

"You shall not test the Lord your God, as you tested Him in Massah."

What is meant by "tested God" and "in Massah" no less? We find the answer to that question in the 17th chapter of the book of Exodus[1-7]...

"Then all the congregation of the sons of Israel journeyed by stages from the wilderness of Sin, according to the command of the Lord, and camped at Rephidim, and there was no water for the people to drink. Therefore the people quarreled with Moses and said, 'Give us water that we may drink.' And Moses said to them, 'Why do you quarrel with me? Why do you test the Lord? But the people thirsted there for water; and they grumbled against Moses and said, 'Why, now, have you brought us up from Egypt, to kill us and our children and our livestock with thirst?" So Moses cried out to the Lord, saying, 'What shall I do to this people? A little more and they will stone me.' Then the Lord said to Moses, 'Pass before the people and take with you some of the elders of Israel; and take in your hand your staff with which you struck the Nile, and go. Behold, I will stand before you there on the rock at Horeb; and you shall strike the rock, and water will come out of it, that the people may drink.' And Moses did so in the sight of the elders of Israel. And he named the place **Massah** and **Meribah** because of the quarrel of the sons of Israel, and because they tested the Lord, saying...

"Is the Lord among us, or not?"

Recent history is chocked full real life examples of seemingly pious people (children of light) whom after seeking the "secret knowledge" of the occult, ultimately conceded to the conditions of darkness (Aleister Crowley, Alice Bailey, Barbara Mariciniak, Sue Keiffer). All Mankind are created equal. It stands to reason then, that all knowledge that is good and true (of God) would be shared equally also.

"And he called the name of the place Massah, and
Meribah, because of the chiding of the children of
Israel, and because they tempted the LORD, saying, Is
the LORD among us, or not?"

–Exodus 17:7

The words Massah (מַסָּה) and Meribah (מְרִיבָה) in Hebrew literally translates to indicate both a place in the desert and respectively to "test" and "provoke." How strongly does Mosaic Law forbid attempts to force the hand of God?

"Ye shall not tempt the LORD your God, as ye tempted
him in Massah."

–Deuteronomy 6:16

"And at Taberah, and at Massah, and at
Kibrothhattaavah, ye provoked the LORD to wrath."

–Deuteronomy 9:22

"And of Levi he said, Let thy Thummim and thy Urim be
with thy holy one, whom thou didst prove at Massah, and
with whom thou didst strive at the waters of Meribah;"

–Deuteronomy 33:8

It seems safe to assume that the God of the Hebrews does not concede to incessant appeal for favor or of proofs.

"Woe to those who draw sin along with cords of deceit, and wickedness as with cart ropes, to those who say, 'Let God hurry,' let Him hasten His work so that we may see it. Let it approach, let the plan of the Holy One of Israel come, so we may know it."

–Isaiah 5:18,19

Some religionists even today, expect of their leaders, certain working of miracles as proof that "God is with them." But Jesus made it known to the "Benny Hinns" of his day that their fraudulent works of darkness will be brought to light.

"Beware ye of the leaven of the Pharisees, which is hypocrisy. For there is nothing covered, that shall not be revealed; neither hid, that shall not be known. Therefore whatsoever ye have spoken in darkness shall be heard in the light; and that which ye have spoken in the ear in closets shall be proclaimed upon the housetops.

–Luke 12:1-3; Matthew 10:26

The only thing that the workings of the occult prove to the secular Christian is charlatanism. For such rational minded folk, the point is not whether "a just and merciful God exists" but would she concede to "such an act as this?"

The Third Temptation

After Jesus rebukes the Spirit of Pride by refusing to throw himself from the ledge of a mountain, he is tempted again. From such height, it's as if Jesus can see all the great municipalities...

The Spirit of Lust. All this yours for the taking, if you will fall down and worship Me.

From a purely rational perspective, we can identify with Jesus standing at the top of a high place overlooking the hustle and bustle of the towns below. As he reflects on the progress of his spiritual journey, the ego slyly slithers back in through the back door as if to say, "All of these people do my work for naught. But you are special, Work for me and experience success and happiness beyond your wildest dreams.

Jesus: Get away from me evil spirit, for it is written, "Thou shalt worship the Lord thy God, and Him only shalt thou serve."

Like many of the today's TV evangelists, Jesus could have cashed in on his rare spiritual acuity. Seemingly selfless people make charismatic rulers with unlimited leadership potential. Once again however, Jesus called on scripture for spiritual sustenance.

Although tempted to "seem" rather than to "be," Jesus empathized with his enslaved brethren as they desperately labored in vain to satisfy their unquenchable thirst for material wealth and status. With conviction, Jesus finalized his resolve as if to say, "One cannot serve both the Spirit and the flesh. It is decided. I would prefer to serve by the light of truth than to rule under the cloak of darkness. Love is its own reward." In real life, the temptations of the spirit are much more subtle than the devil (personification of evil). A fully sane person isn't likely to be confronted by a cantankerous deity who offers them the world in exchange for their soul. But Mankind worships more idols than ever before and no one seems to question it. When Moses came down from Mt. Sinai with the Ten Commandments in hand, he found that the Israelites had fashioned a golden calf (in the traditions of the Egyptian's who for 400 years made them slaves!) and they said...

"This is your god, O Israel, that brought you out of the land of Egypt."

-Exodus 32:4

In this age of technology of course, we're too "enlightened" for Apis and the Phoenician Baal (the Egyptian God's of strength and fertility). But our idols are still made of metal and stone, only in the shape of cars, boats, and four car garages and our God is status.

Today's religionists devour the flesh of innocent creatures even in their churches which bear the name of the world's most infamous activist for compassion and the abolition of hypocrisy! Jesus, like Moses (Exodus 34:28) and Elijah (1 Kings 19:8) before him, return from a 40 day fast with radical vision for a new world. Only, he didn't come down from the mountain with a stone tablet in his hand. His philosophy could be summed up with five words: "Love thy neighbor as thyself." From that, the fundamentalist Christian retains nothing. Rather than fashioning a Golden Calf, they kneel before the likeness of Jesus himself.

"Because that, when they knew God, they glorified him not as God, neither were thankful; but became vain in their imaginations, and their foolish heart was darkened. *Professing themselves to be wise, they became fools, And changed the glory of the uncorruptible God into an image made like to corruptible man*, and to birds, and fourfooted beasts, and creeping things."

–Romans 1:21–23

Fundamentalists Christian's are similar to the ancient Israelites in that profess to believe one thing and do another. They worship graven images despite the explicit scriptures forbidding it. They support war, yet their God clearly says "Thou shalt not kill."

We don't fight for the protection of liberties. Rather, we trade the blood of our youths for oil. To kill one's enemies, domestic or abroad is premeditated murder. And what of the fundamentalist Christian who mocks the vegan lifestyle saying,

"The Bible says… the animals are here for us to eat."

Does that mean their God endorses genocide too?

"This is what the Lord Almighty says ... 'Now go and strike Amalek and devote to destruction all that they have. Do not spare them, but kill both man and woman, child and infant, ox and sheep, camel and donkey.' "

–1 Samuel 15.3

What little boy hasn't wondered about Genesis 22 which records Abraham thinking that God told him to murder his son as a sacrificial offering?

"And Abraham took the wood of the burnt offering, and laid it upon Isaac his son; and he took the fire in his hand, and a knife; and they went both of them together."

–Genesis 22.6

How would Man's God fashioned in his own image, prefer his flesh and blood offering, rare or burned at the stake?

"Do not allow a sorceress to live."

Exodus 22:18

Commercial Christianity insists that the Bible is the literal word of God. As such, it should be followed to the letter. Yet they, permit their mothers and daughters to speak.

"I do not permit a woman to teach or to have authority over a man, she must be silent."

–1 Timothy 2:12

Is abortion okay?

"Happy is he who repays you for what you have done to us. He who seizes your infants and dashes them against the rocks."

–Psalm 137

What father reads to his little girl Ephesians 5:22 where it says that women to submit to their husbands?

Never mind, most every male fundamentalist harps on that one...

"Wives, submit yourselves unto your own husbands, as unto the Lord."

–Ephesians 5:22

We know too well, the priest's stance on homosexuality?

"In the same way also the men, giving up natural intercourse with women, were consumed with passion for one another. Men committed shameless acts with men and received in their own persons the due penalty for their error."

–Romans 1:27

The following verse, I hear, was a favorite before the Civil War...

"Slaves, submit yourselves to your masters with all respect, not only to the good and gentle but also to the cruel."

–1 Peter 2:18

Shouldn't we expect the hypocrite to similarly use the Bible to justify his urge to eat the flesh of innocent, albeit defenseless creatures?

I'll stop here, but the point I'm trying to make is an important one. The Bible should be used only as a source of personal inspiration. Because it is most often used by commercial religionists to justify immoral acts the Bible has regretfully become a hindrance of the Kingdom rather than the advance of it. Perhaps the Essenes were on to something in regarding themselves the keepers of secrets after all. The "sWord" as it turns out, can be wielded by the "children of darkness" as well as the "children of light.

Unfortunately, real-life temptations are more subtle than a bribe from the "devil" himself and the line between right and wrong is getting more and more blurred by the ever invasive influence of dissolute media. In times of uncertainty, Jesus called on the scripture for spiritual substance. *In no way however, did he idolize or give the "Word" authority over him*. Jesus refused the biding of any master, other than a righteous and merciful God.

"Thou shalt worship the Lord thy God, and Him only shalt thou serve."

-Matthew 4:8-10

We too should call on the wisdom of our forefathers. But we must first rely on the powers of logic and reason to separate what is good and true from what is not. Only from a strong moral and ethical foundation, may we remain faithful through the trials ahead.

"And the rain descended, and the floods came, and the winds blew, and beat upon that house; and it fell. and great was the fall of it. And it came to pass, when Jesus had ended these sayings, the people were astonished at his doctrine. For he taught them as one having authority, and not as the scribes."

–Matthew 7.27–29

It is important to mention that Jesus wasn't the only entity in the proverbial desert who called on the scripture to justify their position. In Matthew [4:5-7], we find that the "devil" recites Psalm [91:9-12]:

"Because thou hast made the LORD, which is my refuge, even the most High, thy habitation; There shall no evil befall thee, neither shall any plague come nigh thy dwelling. For he shall give his angels charge over thee, to keep thee in all thy ways. They shall bear thee up in their hands, lest thou dash thy foot against a stone. "

–Psalms 91.9–12

Had Jesus not exercised rational sense in calling on Deuteronomy 6:16, you wouldn't be reading this.

"And they were astonished at his doctrine: for he taught them as one that had authority, and not as the scribes."

–Mark 1:22

"For I say unto you, That except your righteousness shall exceed the righteousness of the scribes and Pharisees, ye shall in no case enter into the kingdom of heaven."

–Matthew 5:20

"And all they in the synagogue, when they heard these things, were filled with wrath, And rose up, and thrust him out of the city, and led him unto the brow of the hill whereon their city was built, that they might cast him down headlong. But he passing through the midst of them went his way, And came down to Capernaum, a city of Galilee, and taught them on the sabbath days. And they were astonished at his doctrine: for his word was with power. "

–Luke 4:28–32

"The prophet that hath a dream, let him tell a dream; and he that hath my word, let him speak my word faithfully. What is the chaff to the wheat? saith the LORD. Is not my word like as a fire? saith the LORD; and like a hammer that breaketh the rock in pieces?"

-Jeremiah 23:28-29

"When the righteous are in authority, the people rejoice: but when the wicked beareth rule, the people mourn."

-Proverbs 29:2

"Every wise woman buildeth her house: but the foolish plucketh it down with her hands. He that walketh in his uprightness feareth the LORD: but **he that is perverse in his ways despiseth him. In the mouth of the foolish is a rod of pride:** but the lips of the wise shall preserve them. Where no oxen are, the crib is clean: but much increase is by the strength of the ox. **A faithful witness will not lie:** but a false witness will utter lies. A scorner seeketh wisdom, and findeth it not: but **knowledge is easy unto him that understandeth.** Go from the presence of a foolish man, when thou perceivest not in him the lips of knowledge. **The wisdom of the prudent is to understand his way:** but the folly of fools is deceit. Fools make a mock at sin: but among the righteous there is favour. The heart knoweth his own bitterness; and a stranger doth not intermeddle with his joy. The house of the wicked shall be overthrown: but the tabernacle of the upright shall flourish. There is a way which seemeth right unto a man, but the end thereof are the ways of death. Even in laughter the heart is sorrowful; and the end of that mirth is heaviness. The backslider in heart shall be filled with his own ways: and a good man shall be satisfied from himself. **The simple believeth every word: but the prudent man looketh well to his going.** A wise man feareth, and departeth from evil: but the fool rageth, and is confident. He that is soon angry dealeth foolishly: and a man of wicked devices is hated. **The simple inherit folly: but the prudent are crowned with knowledge.** The evil bow before the good; and the wicked at the gates of the righteous. **The poor is hated even of his own neighbour: but the rich hath many friends. He that despiseth his neighbour sinneth: but he that hath mercy on the poor, happy is he. Do they not err that devise evil? but mercy and truth shall be to them that devise good.** In all labour there is profit: but the talk of the lips tendeth only to penury. The crown of the wise is their riches; but the foolishness of fools is folly. A true witness delivereth souls; but a deceitful witness speaketh lies. In the fear of the LORD is strong confidence; and his children shall have a place of refuge. The fear of the LORD is a fountain of life, to depart from the snares of death. In the multitude of people is the king's honour; but in the want of people is the destruction of the prince. He that is slow to wrath is of great understanding; but he that is hasty of spirit exalteth folly. A sound heart is the life of the flesh; but envy the rottenness of the bones. **He that oppresseth the poor reproacheth his Maker; but he that honoureth him hath mercy on the poor.** The wicked is driven away in his wickedness; but the righteous hath hope in his death. **Wisdom resteth in the heart of him that hath understanding;** but that which is in the midst of fools is made known. Righteousness exalteth a nation; but sin is a reproach to any people."

–Proverbs 14:1–34

Having unreservedly denounced the pleasures of the flesh, the temptations ceased and Jesus fully realized the true significance of a Kingdom at peace. He emerged from the wilderness to share the experience with John. From there, Jesus departs to begin his ministry...

John the prophet: Behold the Lamb of God.

Hearing this, two of John's followers approach Jesus.

Jesus: What do you seek?

John's followers: where are you staying?.

Jesus: Come and see

The men listened in awe as Jesus' shared his profound insights until late in the evening. Andrew (one of the two followers of John) returned home to tell his brother Simon that he had found their long awaited messiah that would finally free them from the tyranny of Rome. But when Simon met him, he resolved immediately to commit his life to Jesus' vision of a kingdom at peace. From then on, Jesus called him Peter (Cephas, which means "stone"). On the way to Galilee, Jesus met Philip a neighboring villager of Andrew and Peter. Philip and his brother Nathanael also became disciples of Jesus.

Jesus returned to Nazareth on holiday and went to the Assembly. He was called upon to read from the book of Isaiah from which he recited chapter 61, verses 1-3:

"The Spirit of the Lord GOD is within me; because the LORD hath anointed me to preach good tidings unto the meek; he hath sent me to bind up the brokenhearted, to proclaim liberty to the captives, and the opening of the prison to them that are bound; To proclaim the acceptable Age (שָׁנָה) of the LORD, and the day of reckoning (נָקָם) of our God; to comfort all that mourn; To appoint unto them that mourn in Zion, to give unto them beauty for ashes, the oil of joy for mourning, the garment of praise for the spirit of heaviness; that they might be called trees of righteousness, the planting of the LORD, that he might be glorified.

Jesus closed the book, gave it back to the minister and sat down. The eyes of everyone in the synagogue were fastened on him. Jesus returned the book to the attendant, and sat down. His disciples eagerly awaited his response...

Jesus: That scripture is being fulfilled this very day.

Service not Sacrifice

On a day traditionally set aside for the Sabbath, Jesus and his followers plucked some corn as they walked across a field. Some religionist noticed them rubbing the ears to prepare them for eating...

Religionist: Anyone who works on the Sabbath should be stoned to death, according to the law that God had given to Moses.

Jesus: You would not condemn what is harmless if you understood that a compassionate God requires love and mercy NOT sacrifice.

The spirit of fear and trepidation continued to tempt Jesus and his followers even after his ascension in the wilderness. But Jesus would not submit. Neither should we be intimidated by any person, no matter how rich, educated or otherwise imposing. Jesus stood before the experts and the most respected religious and political officials of the law, only to treat them as students. True wisdom is attained through selfless acts of service minded compassion. The experience of oneness with the Spirit of God requires that we put our trust in it. True Christianity is the practice of loving without regard for self-interests.

On another occasion of the Sabbath, Jesus was approached by a sick woman. An elder of the church noticed Jesus comforting her...

Church elder. There are six days in the week on which to work.

Jesus. Do you think it is wrong to honor God on the Sabbath?

At a loss for words, the experts did not answer.

Jesus. Hypocrites! Who among you refuses to release his ox from its manger and lead it to water on the Sabbath?

"And if your sheep fell into a well, which one would not pull it out, even on the Sabbath?"

"You hold yourselves in higher esteem than a sheep. Yet you say it is wrong to help a Man... What then do you think we should do on the Sabbath: good or evil? Nourish the sick or disregard them? Always do good works, even on the Sabbath."

The Perfect Time and Place

God has put us in the perfect position of time and place to advance the Kingdom. Often however, the best opportunities seem the most ill-timed. Consider your next encounter with a particularly antagonistic individual. This person might be under the influence of a chemical substance (drugs, alcohol, adrenaline etc.). Perhaps they have a lowly reputation and because of that, we may feel embarrassed to associate with them. It is by these occasions that the flesh may nourish the spirit...

Jesus saw a tax collector by the name of Matthew receiving taxes. Remember that tax collectors, were employed by occupying Rome. They were loathed by their fellow Jews. Interaction with them meant excommunication and isolation from "polite" society. It's hard to imagine the insufferable way these social "lepers" were treated by their more devout socially esteemed counterparts. But Jesus greeted Matthew with the same level of honor and respect as he did the high priest.

Understandably, Matthew must have felt obligated. He invited Jesus into his home and introduced him to some of his friends and fellow tax collectors who had also been excluded from the religionist community. Jesus and his disciples lovingly broke bread with them.

Mark [2:17] tells us that when the Religionist see Jesus in the company of sinners, they questioned his disciples...

Religionists: How is it that your teacher eats with tax collectors and nonbelievers? (The Church forbade interaction with them.)

Jesus: They that are whole have no need of the physician, but they that are sick: I came not to call the righteous, but sinners to repentance.

But in Matthew 15:1-24 Jesus is confronts a different line of questioning and quickly responds...

Religionists: Why does your group transgress the tradition of the elders by not washing their hands before they eat?

Jesus: Why do you disobey the commandment of God by in favor of the traditions of your people? For one of God's commandments say "Honor your father and mother: and anyone who curses his father or mother is to be put to death." And yet, by your customs, it's acceptable to say, "I give to the church a dedicatory gift in place of what I should be giving to my Parents."

Jesus continues: So by your temple traditions, you break God's law and neglect to care for your parents. Are these not the superficial acts that the prophet Isaiah spoke? You hypocrites! Isaiah prophesied well concerning you, saying, 'This people profess with their mouth, and with their lips that they honor me, but their heart is far from me. They worship vainly, teaching as doctrines the commandments of men."

According to the following passage, Jesus was not privy to the hygienic importance of washing one's hands and eating utensils. He called out to the bystanders saying...

"Listen to this and understand: it is not that which goes into the mouth which defiles a man, but that which comes out."

Not surprisingly, Jesus' disciples pulled him aside...

"Do you not realize that Pharisees were offended by what you said back there?"

Note: Such a response indicates Jesus felt slighted by the religionists and (as we all do) broke his own decree not to "resist an evil"...

Jesus: "Every plant which my heavenly father did not sow will be uprooted. Do not concern yourself with them. They are but blind guides of the blind. If a blind man leads a blind man, both will fall in a pit."

Remember Jesus' whole harangue was instigated from someone simply asking why he and his disciples didn't washing their hands before eating bread! Understandably, Peter asks Jesus to explain...

Jesus: Do you too still lack understanding? Everything that goes into the mouth proceeds into the stomach and is discharged into the latrine? But the things which come out of the mouth come from the depths of the heart, and those things defile a man.

I've heard all kinds of religionist restructurings of what Jesus might have meant to say here. But the Bible records that he was given multiple opportunities to rescind, yet he repeated this nugget of "wisdom" for the sake of posterity. Jesus was simply a man unaware of the hygienic benefits of this custom. If he had been the embodiment of a loving all-knowing God (as so the commercial religionists claim) however, he would not have condemned such a lifesaving practice as the washing of hands before eating.

The preceding passage is reminiscent of Jesus' running up to a fig tree and seeing that it had no fruit: he cursed at it...

"And on the morrow, when they were come from Bethany, he was hungry: And seeing a fig tree afar off having leaves, he came, if haply he might find any thing thereon: and when he came to it, he found nothing but leaves; for the time of figs was not yet. And Jesus answered and said unto it, No man eat fruit of thee hereafter for ever. And his disciples heard it. "

–Mark 11:12-14

Many evangelists have used Jesus' cursing of the fig tree as a parable about fruitless forms of worship. But the two preceding accounts seem to me, like authentic events, maybe someone's favorite accounts of an old friend. One can't help but smile to imagine one of Jesus' disciples affectionately reminiscing. Sadly, such joy is lost on the commercial religionist who wishes only to deify history's most celebrated activist. Obviously, the canonical Gospels have been authored by multiple "evangelists." Mark 2:17 and Matthew 15:1-24 describe very different versions of what appear to be the same event same event. Matthew 9:9-38 submits an ever more intimate rendering...

Matthew writes: Jesus saw me sitting at the tax desk, and he said "Follow me." Immediately, I got up and followed him. After some time, Jesus and his disciples and I were ministering in my home. When some of the Pharisees saw us, they said of the disciples, "Why does your master eat with the tax-collectors and sinners?" Jesus overheard this and said to them, "Those who boast of good health refuse the services of a doctor. But these people are openly ill." Go and learn what this means: "I desire mercy and not sacrifice." For I have not come to call the righteous, but the sinners to repentance.

Sometime after this, John's disciples came to Jesus asking, "Why do we and the Pharisees fast often, but your disciples do not?" Jesus said to them, "Surely the wedding guests do not mourn while the bridegroom remains with them? But the days will come when the bridegroom will be taken away from, and then they will fast. No man putteth a piece of new cloth unto an old garment, for that which is put in to fill it up taketh from the garment, and the rent is made worse. Neither do men put new wine into old bottles: else the bottles break, and the wine runneth out, and the bottles perish: but they put new wine into new bottles, and both are preserved."

According to this account, Jesus didn't waste a lot of time trying to persuade people as to the merits of ministry. He simply asked Matthew to join him and he did so without a moment's hesitation. Again, you simply cannot say the wrong thing to the right person. Obviously, Jesus wasn't one to hesitate either. He shared his gospel with anyone who would accept it. In the spirit of truth, there are no saints; only sinners and hypocrites. The self-righteous proclaim either that there IS (religionists) or isn't (atheist) a supernatural and therefore base their actions accordingly. Only the meek, who with humbled hearts openly admit that they are sinners, can see the significance of advancing a better world regardless of outcome.

To the hypocritical religionists with their superficial and misguided forms of worship, Jesus quoted his beloved scripture.

For I desired mercy, and not sacrifice; and the knowledge of God more than burnt offerings. But they like men have transgressed the covenant: there have they dealt treacherously against me.

–Hosea 6:6-7

"Hear the word of the LORD, ye rulers of Sodom; give ear unto the law of our God, ye people of Gomorrah. To what purpose is the multitude of your sacrifices unto me? saith the LORD: I am full of the burnt offerings of rams, and the fat of fed beasts; and **I delight not in the blood of bullocks, or of lambs, or of the goats.** When ye come to appear before me, who hath required this at your hand, to tread my courts? **Bring no more vain oblations;** incense is an abomination unto me; the new moons and sabbaths, the calling of assemblies, I cannot away with; it is iniquity, even the solemn meeting. Your new moons and your appointed feasts my soul hateth: they are a trouble unto me; I am weary to bear them. And when ye spread forth your hands, I will hide mine eyes from you: yea, **when ye make many prayers, I will not hear: your hands are full of blood. Wash you, make you clean; put away the evil of your doings from before mine eyes; cease to do evil; Learn to do well; seek judgment, relieve the oppressed,** judge the fatherless, plead for the widow. **Come now, and let us reason together,** saith the LORD: though your sins be as scarlet, they shall be as white as snow; though they be red like crimson, they shall be as wool."

Isaiah 1.10–18

He judged the cause of the poor and needy; then it was well with him; was not this to know me? saith the LORD. But thine eyes and thine heart are not but for thy covetousness, and for to shed innocent blood, and for oppression, and for violence, to do it.

–Jeremiah 22.16–17

Wherewith shall I come before the LORD, and bow myself before the high God? shall I come before him with burnt offerings, with calves of a year old? Will the LORD be pleased with thousands of rams, or with ten thousands of rivers of oil? shall I give my firstborn for my transgression, the fruit of my body for the sin of my soul? He hath shewed thee, O man, what is good; and what doth the LORD require of thee, but to do justly, and to love mercy, and to walk humbly with thy God?

–Micah 6.6–8

"Every way of a man is right in his own eyes; but the LORD pondereth the hearts. To do justice and judgment is more acceptable to the LORD than sacrifice. An high look, and a proud heart, and the plowing of the wicked, is sin. "

Proverbs 21.2–4

I want to point out again, that some of John's disciples come by asking Jesus why he and his disciples do not fast like everyone else. Jesus' answer indicates that they have no reason to mourn superficially for that time will in due season.

"Surely the wedding guests do not mourn while the bridegroom is still with them? But the days will come when the bridegroom will be taken away from them, and then they will fast."

In this way, Jesus explains that fasting for the sake of suffering has no merit. But the appetite curbs as a natural response to suffering and in this way, both the old and new traditions of each Age are preserved.

"No man putteth a piece of new cloth unto an old garment, for that which is put in to fill it up taketh from the garment, and the rent is made worse. Neither do men put new wine into old bottles; else the bottles break, and the wine runneth out, and the bottles perish; but they put new wine into new bottles, and both are preserved."

–Mathew 9:13–17

The True "House" of God

The commercial religionists of Jesus' time considered Jerusalem to be the holiest of holies. They believed in fact, that God literally dwelt within the walls of their temple. John 2:16 tells us that Jesus went there during Passover and quoting a special blend of scripture Isaiah 56:5-11; Jeremiah 7:11; Hosea 12:7-8 in protest to the selling of animals to be sacrificed at the temple alter...

Jesus: "Take these things hence; make not my Father's house a house of merchandise."

On more than one occasion, Jesus went to the courts of the temple protesting sacrificial offerings. The priests had programmed their parishioners that God sanctioned the merchandizing of these select animals and doves to be butchered (again, at the temple alter) as a prayer offering to God! It must have been an especially gruesome affair. But Jesus drove out the animals and scattered the blood-money on the ground. It is a chilling depiction of activism to picture Jesus in the midst of the priests protesting the profiteering of innocent creatures under the guise of sacrifice to a barbaric God. Are we to believe that he protested only the fundraising?

"For I desired mercy, and not sacrifice; and the knowledge of God more than burnt offerings."

–Hosea 6:6

To Never Thirst

On another occasion, while passing through Samaria, Jesus sat down by Jacob's well to rest while his disciples went into the town to fetch bread. A local woman came to draw water, and he asked her for a drink...

Woman by the well: How is it that you ask me for a drink of water? (Ordinarily, Jews would have no contact with Samaritans.)

Jesus: If you knew of my teachings, you would not have said that. For whoever drinks of this well will thirst again. But whoever partakes of that from which I speak will be a well of water in him, springing up into everlasting life from which he shall never thirst again.

Woman by the well: I feel that you are sincere, but how can you teach me when you are a Jew and I am a Samaritan? My people pray to God upon this mountain, but your people say that the true house of God is only in Jerusalem.

Jesus: The time has come when people will look neither to the mountain nor to Jerusalem. They will serve the Kingdom of God by their works rather than superficial rites.

To Never Hunger

The book of John [4:31-38] tells us that after sharing the Gospel of the Kingdom with the Samaritan woman at the well, Jesus' felt physically gratified...

Disciples: Rabbi, eat something.

Jesus: I have food to eat which you do not know of.

At this point the disciples began to speak amongst themselves, "Has someone brought him anything to eat?"

Jesus: My sustenance is in doing the will of the one that sent me, and complete my mission. Do you not say, 'It is still four months for the harvest to come?'" Behold, I tell you, lift up your eyes and look at the fields for they are already white and ready for the harvest. And the reaper receives wages and gathers fruit unto life eternal, so that the sower and the reaper rejoice together. For in this matter the saying is true, that the sower is one and the reaper another. I have sent you to reap that which you did not toil over. Others have labored, but you have entered into their charge."

In fulfilling or serving our life's purpose, we receive the fruits of that which we ourselves have not sown. In this way we nourish the Spirit in happy communion with the great servants who came before us.

On yet another occasion, one of the Religionist invited Jesus to dinner. When Jesus entered, he sat down without washing his hands. Jesus noticing that he had stunned his host used the situation to make a point...

Jesus: You blind Pharisee, cleanse first that which is within the cup and platter that the outside of them may be clean also.

Above all, be merciful and compassionate. Only then, may the rest be clean. The book of Luke[7:37-39] reports that a woman known for her transgressions came to the aristocrat's home carrying an alabaster box. (See also, pgs. 297 & 301) As they talked, she knelt at his feet and cried. She dried the tears with her hair. After witnessing Jesus allow the "desecrated" woman to touch him, the religionist host began to doubt Jesus' wholesomeness. Again, Jesus noticed the dismay of his host.

Jesus: Shall I tell you what I believe is happening here?

Religionist host: Yes, please!

Jesus: There were two men who held themselves debtors to one master, one for five hundred pieces of silver and the other for fifty. *Seeing that neither of them had any means to pay; their creditor forgave them both. Which of them do you think would love his master and care for him most?*

Religionist host: He that owed the most, of course.

Jesus to the host: So it is with you and this woman. You consider yourself devout and therefore a small debtor. She acknowledges her transgressions and thus considers herself to be a great debtor. I came into your house and you did not give me water to wash my feet; she washes them with her tears and wipes them with her hair. You did not even kiss my cheek or anoint my head with oil, yet she anoints my feet with her tears. He who considers himself devout will not perform such acts of humble adoration. It is by the same measure that this woman humbles herself however, that she is exalted.

Note: The astute reader of the Gospels cannot help but notice that the authors of Matthew 1:16; 1:18; 1:20; 2:11; 13:55; 27:56; 27:61; 28:1; Luke 1:27; 1:30; 1:34; 1:38; 1:39; 1:41; 1:46; 1:56; 2:5; 2:16; 2:19; 2:34; 8:2; 10:39; 10:42; 24:10; and John 11:1; 11:2; 11:19; 11:20; 11:28; 11:31; 11:32; 11:45; 12:3; 19:25; 20:1; 20:11; 20:16; 20:18 make innumerable references to women named "Mary," while Mark 6:3; 15:40; 15:47; 16:1; 16:9 (most likely the earliest if not original of the three accounts) makes only five. You'll soon find that I could not merge these instances, even in this synopsis because of timeline differences. From a purely psychological perspective, it seems obvious that these early evangelist authors needed to circumvent a political agenda surrounding Jesus and a certain woman named Mary.

Jesus addressing his host: One cannot think too highly of himself and be loving and merciful at the same time. Listen to this, "Two men came into the Temple to pray. One was a religionist, and the other a tax-collector. The religionist prayed:

> "I thank thee O' God that I am not miserly, nor a libertine, nor a deceiver, nor such a wretch as a tax-collector or a sinner. I fast twice a week, and give away a tenth of my property. But the tax-collector stood far away, and dared not look up to heaven but only beat his breast, praying God please be merciful to me a sinner."

Jesus continues: The tax collector's prayer is sincere, for he who exalts himself is demeaned in the presence of God. But He who humbles himself will glorifies God and is thereby Himself exalted.

In this way, Jesus taught the true meaning of love and mercy. We should be ever mindful of our intentions for salvation will not come with self-righteous indignation.

Seemingly immune to the estimations of others, Jesus accepted without judgment, anyone who would hear his teachings. Even good works are of no merit, should one's intentions be to raise himself up in the eyes of others. For what good is a higher rung in a ladder we wish to cut down. As activists, we wish to change the world for the better. But how can we expect to teach that which we ourselves do not know?

"But whereunto shall I liken this generation? It is like unto children sitting in the markets, and calling unto their fellows, And saying, **We have piped unto you, and ye have not danced; we have mourned unto you, and ye have not lamented**. For John came neither eating nor drinking, and they say, He hath a devil. I came eating and drinking, and they say, Behold a man gluttonous, and a winebibber, a friend of publicans and sinners. But wisdom is justified of her children."

–Matthew 11.16–19

Predominantly no one wants to listen to activists' rant because we have been like Jesus' self-righteous host in that our motives have been mixed. We must be mindful of our true intentions either to be a voice for the voiceless or simply to prove the righteousness of our stance on animal rights. Love and mercy have nothing to do with status.

"Beware of the scribes, which desire to walk in long robes, and love greetings in the markets, and the highest seats in the synagogues, and the chief rooms at feasts; Which devour widows' houses, and for show make long prayers; the same shall receive greater damnation."

–Luke 20:46–47

We should do nothing to put on airs for the sake of appearances. Jesus taught his followers that it is better "to be" rather than to seem. The old teachings of external rites and judgment toward others cannot be combined with Jesus' teachings of love and compassion. One cannot strive both for the Kingdom and for the glory of Men no more righteous than ourselves. Those who choose the late must either abandon the first and resort to violence or fail miserably.

"Man has always desired power. Ownership of property gives this power. Man hankers also after posthumous fame based on power."

–Gandhi

Later on, some of John's disciples came to Jesus seeking reassurance that the ministry would go on after his death. He had been imprisoned by Herod and was awaiting execution...

Jesus: Go and tell John again those things which you have seen and heard here today. The blind receive sight and the deaf now hear; the lame walk and the dead are raised; the poor of spirit are ministered to and the unclean are purified. And blessed is he, who is not be offended by these works.

Jesus sent the disciples back to John so that he would be reassured. Then he began to edify his mentor in the presence of the crowd.

Jesus: When you went in search of John in the wilderness, what did you go to find? A reed shaken by the wind? What did you expect to see? A man clothed in soft raiment? Those who wear soft clothing minister in kings' houses. Then what do you venture to see? A prophet? Yes, but I assure you that John was much more than that. For this is John, of whom it is written...

"Comfort, comfort my people, says your God. Speak tenderly to Jerusalem, and cry to her that her warfare is ended, that her iniquity is pardoned, that she has received from the LORD's hand double for all her sins. A voice cries: "In the wilderness prepare the way of the LORD; make straight in the desert a highway for our God. Every valley shall be lifted up, and every mountain and hill be made low; the uneven ground shall become level, and the rough places a plain. And the glory of the LORD shall be revealed, and all flesh shall see it together, for the mouth of the LORD has spoken." A voice says, "Cry!" And I said, "What shall I cry?" All flesh is grass, and all its beauty is like the flower of the field. The grass withers, the flower fades when the breath of the LORD blows on it; surely the people are grass. The grass withers, the flower fades, but the word of our God will stand forever. Go on up to a high mountain, O Zion, herald of good news; lift up your voice with strength, O Jerusalem, herald of good news; lift it up, fear not; say to the cities of Judah, "Behold your God!" Behold, the Lord GOD comes with might, and his arm rules for him; behold, his reward is with him, and his recompense before him. He will tend his flock like a shepherd; he will gather the lambs in his arms; he will carry them in his bosom, and gently lead those that are with young. Who has measured the waters in the hollow of his hand and marked off the heavens with a span, enclosed the dust of the earth in a measure and weighed the mountains in scales and the hills in a balance? Who has measured the Spirit of the LORD, or what man shows him his counsel? Whom did he consult, and who made him understand? Who taught him the path of justice, and taught him knowledge, and showed him the way of understanding? Behold, the nations are like a drop from a bucket, and are accounted as the dust on the scales; behold, he takes up the coastlands like fine dust. Lebanon would not suffice for fuel, nor are its beasts enough for a burnt offering. All the nations are as nothing before him, they are accounted by him as less than nothing and emptiness. To whom then will you liken God, or what likeness compare with him? An idol! A craftsman casts it, and a goldsmith overlays it with gold and casts for it silver chains. He who is too impoverished for an offering chooses wood that will not rot; he seeks out a skillful craftsman to set up an idol that will not move. Do you not know? Do you not hear? Has it not been told you from the beginning? Have you not understood from the foundations of the earth? It is he who sits above the circle of the earth, and its inhabitants are like grasshoppers; who stretches out the heavens like a curtain, and spreads them like a tent to dwell in; who brings princes to nothing, and makes the rulers of the earth as emptiness. Scarcely are they planted, scarcely sown, scarcely has their stem taken root in the earth, when he blows on them, and they wither, and the tempest carries them off like stubble. To whom then will you compare me, that I should be like him? says the Holy One. Lift up your eyes on high and see: who created these? He who brings out their host by number, calling them all by name, by the greatness of his might, and because he is strong in power not one is missing. Why do you say, O Jacob, and speak, O Israel, "My way is hidden from the LORD, and my right is disregarded by my God"? Have you not known? Have you not heard? The LORD is the everlasting God, the Creator of the ends of the earth. He does not faint or grow weary; his understanding is unsearchable. He gives power to the faint, and to him who has no might he increases strength. Even youths shall faint and be weary, and young men shall fall exhausted; but they who wait for the LORD shall renew their strength; they shall mount up with wings like eagles; they shall run and not be weary; they shall walk and not faint."

Isaiah 40.1-31

Jesus. He that hath ears to hear, let him hear. But whereunto shall I liken this generation? They are like children in the street who chatter to one another and wonder why their words carry no substance. They judge a man's worth by his status in the eyes of Men rather than by his merit, consistency of words and conviction of his deeds. For John came neither eating nor drinking, and they say, He hath a devil. I came eating and drinking, and they say, Behold a man gluttonous, and a winebibber, a friend of publicans and sinners. But wisdom is justified of her children. You did not go into the wilderness to see a religionist dressed in rich man's clothes, such men live here in the palaces. What then, did you wish to see in the wilderness? Did you go there because you think John is one of the great prophets? Do not think so; John is not like the others. His words are truer than all the others' measured together.

It is important to remember that the prominent teachers of Mosaic Law went to see John too. But they did not understand the value of his teachings, choosing rather to write him off as a man of no importance. They were like wolves in sheep's clothing. Such religionists consider relevant, only that which exalt themselves in the eyes of Men. Of the teachings on love and equality, they no nothing. Outwardly, they look good and smell good. Inwardly, they stench of death. Of what John taught, they learned only that he fasted in the wilderness and had no possessions. Of him they said, "There is a devil in him." Of what Jesus taught, they understood only that he did no longer fasted as the other Jews. The commercial religionists said of Jesus, "He eats and drinks with tax gatherers and sinners. He is of the world." They were used to charlatans and mystics who professed of material riches in the afterlife, but Jesus and John proclaimed that the Kingdom was in their midst...

Religionist: How can we find this blessed place?

Jesus: The prophets of old spoke of a kingdom marked by visible and diverse signs. But the true coming of the Kingdom of God cannot be seen with the eyes. If anyone tells you: "See, it is coming here or there" do not believe them. For there shall arise false Christs, and false prophets, who will show great signs and wonders; insomuch that, if it were possible, they shall deceive the very elect. But be not deceived, the Kingdom of God is within you.

After taking sabbatical in the wilderness, Jesus did not fast, honor the Sabbath, observe external rites of cleanliness (being unaware hygienic value) nor instruct his followers to do so. A prominent ruler and religionist Jew named Nicodemus came to Jesus during the concealment of night. He acknowledged Jesus' sincerity but wanted clarity as to the significance of the Kingdom...

Jesus: Without a new birth no man is able to see the kingdom of God.

Nicodemus: How is it possible for a man to be given birth when he is old? Is he able to go into his mother's body a second time and come to birth again?

Jesus: If a man's birth is not both from water and from the Spirit, it will not possible for him to enter the Kingdom of God. That which has birth from the flesh is of the flesh, and that which has birth from the Spirit is of the spirit. Do not be surprised that you do not understand what I mean in saying "It is necessary for you to have a second birth." The teachings of the Kingdom is like the wind. Its comings and goings seem without course or reason. The sound of it comes to your ears, but you are unable to determine from whence it came nor where it is going. It is the same with those who have been born of the Spirit.

Could it be that Jesus is saying that many bodies, though born of the flesh, have yet to be born of a "soul?" If so, then Jesus regarded the flesh as little more than a lifeless shell until born of the Spirit.

Nicodemus: I still do not understand how it is possible for these things to be?

Jesus: You profess to be the teacher of Israel and have no knowledge of these things? We say that of which we have knowledge; we give witness of what we have seen; and you do not take our witness to be true. If you have no belief when my words are about the things of earth, how will you have belief if my words are about the things of heaven? The light of the Kingdom shines into the world. Yet because their acts are evil, Men have more love for the darkness. The light is hated by everyone whose acts are evil and he does not come to the light for fear that his acts will be seen. But he whose life is true comes into the light, so that it may be clearly seen that his acts have been done with the help of God.

Jesus traveled from town to town, village to village sharing his message of hope. He saw that the people were like sheep without a Shepherd. They toiled in vain to satisfy their insatiable thirst for material riches. It is the same today. Even with all our technological advancements, most of us lead lives of quiet desperation.

"If it is possible for the human tongue to give the fullest description of God, I have come to the conclusion that God is Truth."   –Gandhi

There are some among us who have an intermittent vision of the Kingdom but fail to faithfully serve due to the competing demands of this realm. But we must choose truth or commit to a life of deceit (denial of one's existence) by default. As long as we serve the unequitable concerns of this world, we are but puppets of it; never experiencing what it means to be truly alive. Jesus wanted to share his vision of the Kingdom with as many people as possible. Mostly, it was the poor and downtrodden who came to hear him. The wealthy elite would not receive Jesus because of his insistence that devotees give their riches to the poor. At this point, word of his ministry had grown far and wide. As a large crowd of people began to gather him, Jesus went up on a mount and prepared to deliver the greatest sermon in history…

The Gospel on the Mount

Jesus: Blessed are the poor in spirit for theirs is the kingdom of heaven.

"How beautiful upon the mountains are the feet of him that bringeth good tidings, that publisheth peace; that bringeth good tidings of good, that publisheth salvation; that saith unto Zion, Thy God reigneth!"

-Isaiah 52:7

Note: Jesus refused credit for his teachings. Rather, he says that he relied on the Spirit of God to tell him what to say. In his Sermon on the Mount, Jesus beautifully interweaves ancient Jewish scripture throughout.

Jesus: Blessed are they that mourn; for they shall be comforted.

The Spirit of the Lord GOD is upon me; because the LORD hath anointed me to preach good tidings unto the meek; he hath sent me to bind up the brokenhearted, to proclaim liberty to the captives, and the opening of the prison to them that are bound; To proclaim the acceptable year of the LORD, and the day of vengeance of our God; to comfort all that mourn;

-Isaiah 61:1-2

Jesus: Blessed are the meek: for they shall inherit the earth."

"How beautiful upon the mountains are the feet of him that bringeth good tidings, that publisheth peace; that bringeth good tidings of good, that publisheth salvation; that saith unto Zion, Thy God reigneth!"

-Isaiah 52:7

But the meek shall inherit the earth; and shall delight themselves in the abundance of peace.

-Psalms 37:11

Jesus: Blessed are they which do hunger and thirst after righteousness: for they shall be filled.

The LORD will not suffer the soul of the righteous to famish: but he casteth away the substance of the wicked.

- Proverbs 10:3

Jesus: Blessed are the merciful: for they shall obtain mercy.

With the merciful thou wilt shew thyself merciful; with an upright man thou wilt shew thyself upright;

- -Psalms 18:25

Jesus: Blessed are the pure in heart: for they shall see God. Blessed are the peacemakers: for they shall be called the children of God.

And the work of righteousness shall be peace; and the effect of righteousness quietness and assurance forever.

-   -Isaiah 32:17

Yet the number of the children of Israel shall be as the sand of the sea, which cannot be measured nor numbered; and it shall come to pass, that in the place where it was said unto them, Ye are not my people, there it shall be said unto them, Ye are the sons of the living God.

-   -Hosea 1:10

Jesus: Blessed are they which are persecuted for righteousness' sake: for theirs is the kingdom of heaven. "Blessed are ye, when men shall revile you, and persecute you, and shall say all manner of evil against you falsely, for my sake."

Hearken unto me, ye that know righteousness, the people in whose heart is my law; fear ye not the reproach of men, neither be ye afraid of their revilings.

For the moth shall eat them up like a garment, and the worm shall eat them like wool: but my righteousness shall be for ever, and my salvation from generation to generation.

-Isaiah 51:7

Jesus: Rejoice, and be exceeding glad: for great is your reward in heaven: for so persecuted they the prophets which were before you.

Rejoice with Jerusalem, and be glad with her, all who love her. Rejoice a rejoicing with her, all who mourn for her;

-Isaiah 66:10

Jesus: But I grieve for the rich, for they labor undue and burdensome bounty. Their thirst can never be quenched. In the flesh, they look satisfied but they hunger in Spirit. While in the sight of Man, they rejoice. But they weep in quite solitude. I grieve for those whom everyone praises, for only the greatest of deceivers are praised by the masses. Be not only modest outwardly but also in spirit. Just as salt is good only when it is salty to the taste, the austere life is good only when coupled with humility. So you also, are an example to the world; you are blessed to live an unpretentious life. But if you are poor only outwardly then, like salt that has no savor, your blessing so becomes your plight. Be neither proud; nor ashamed. Ye are the light unto the world. A city that is set on a hill cannot be hid. When a man lights a candle he does not hide under the bench but on the table that it should give light to everyone in the room. Do not conceal your beliefs but let the consistency of your works attest to their value of your convictions. Seeing that you live by the light of truth, others may find their way. By this, do not think that I reject what is good of what is written. My teachings do not breach, but fulfill the requirements of eternal truths. Until the Kingdom of Heaven is manifest on earth, the commandments must be remain.

Jesus' Five Commandments

Commandment One: "Do not Offend"

Jesus: In the Law it is written, "Do not kill… and if one Man kills another, then that Man must be judged…

"But I tell you that any Man who grows angry with another is at fault also. So if you wish to pray to God, first consider your trespasses. Have you spoken abusively to your brother or your sister? If you can think of even one person who feels offended by you, leave your prayers and go first to make peace with them. Then you may pray."

Know that the Kingdom requires neither sacrifice from one Man nor prayer from another, but only peace among them. One cannot contemplate the full significance of the Kingdom if there is a single being towards whom he or she does not feel love. To offend another is to drive the both of you further from God, and thus all of humanity from the Kingdom of Heaven. So this is the first commandment:

"Do not allow yourself to become angry or offend another. If you have spoken harshly to any person, make peace with them so that no one should have a grudge against you."

Commandment Two: "Do not Covet"

Jesus. It is written, "Do not commit adultery… and if you wish to put away your wife, give her a letter of divorcement."

"But I tell you that even a lustful glance is an act of adultery. Do not think that romance is a desirable thing. Sensual desires pervert brotherly love. It is better to renounce the pleasures of the flesh than to lose sight of the Kingdom. But to put away your spouse is to implicate the whole world. For the abandoned are driven to wantonness as well as to those with whom they may unite. So that is the second commandment.

'Do not marry for lust nor for fear of love lost. For the spirit of fear cannot coexist with Love. If you are to be wed, stay with whom you are united, and do not abandon them."

Commandment Three: "Do not take Oaths"

Jesus: In the Old Law it is said, "Do not utter the name of the Lord your God in vain… and do not swear to any untruth To do so is to profane your God."

"But I tell you that every oath is a profanation of God. Therefore, do not swear at all. One cannot promise anything, for the future is wholly in the power of the Spirit. Man cannot turn one hair white or black. How then can He swear beforehand to do one thing or another, and swear to it by God?" But let your communication be, Yea, yea or Nay, nay. For anything more than these words cometh of deciet.

The mind of Man is of very limited capacity and prone to deceit. No person can know the whole truth of any event past, present or future. Should a person feel compelled to take an oath which proves contrary to the will of God, then the oath was evil at inception. Thus every oath is an abomination to God. So the third commandment is:

"Never swear anything before any person. State simply "Yes or "No" to the best of your knowledge."

Commandment Four: "Resist No Evil"

Jesus: Ye have heard that in the Old Law, "An eye for an eye, and a tooth for a tooth." But I say unto you, That you should not fight evil with evil. But whosoever should strike you on the right cheek, turn to him the other also. If any Man should sue you, and take away your coat, let him have your shirt also. And whosoever might compel you to go a mile, go with him two. Give to him that ask of you. And from him that would borrow from you, do not turn away. You have heard it said in the Old Law, "Thou shalt love your neighbor, and hate your enemy." But I say unto you, Love your enemies, bless them that curse you, do good to them that hate you, and pray for them which despitefully use you, and persecute you; That you may be the children of your Father which is in heaven: for he maketh his sun to rise on the evil and on the good, and sendeth rain on the just and on the unjust. For if ye love them which love you, what reward have you? do not even the publicans the same? And if ye salute your brethren only, what do ye more than others? do not even the publicans so? Be ye therefore perfect, even as your Father which is in heaven is perfect.

Again, no mortal man can know the whole of a truth. That is why Jesus asked how one can expect to remove a speck of dust from their brother's eye while there is a twig in his own. Jesus said that no one is perfect but God (the ideal state for which all Men should strive to emulate.) To seek such perfection, though impossible, is the ultimate form of worship.

No person then, in his imperfect state, has a right to stand in judgment of another, especially of perceived wrongs done to himself. Judge not and ye will not be judged. Forgive, and ye will be forgiven. But if you judge others, then by that same standard will you be judged likewise. Those who seek retribution for perceived wrongs are like the morally blind leading the blind. Both inevitably fall into an abyss.

And to what end does one seek retributive justice? A government does not seek to rehabilitate, but only to act on behalf of the potential vigilant, fighting fire with fire. Fines are levied against those accused of thievery. For violent crimes, the state subjects the prisoner (someone's child) to rape, mutilation or even murder's them on behalf of the first victim's family. So, do not expect to find truth and justice in the courts. To entrust one's sense of righteousness to the courts of Men is like throwing precious pearls to the swine who will trample it and tear your sense of decency to pieces in the process. Thus the fifth commandment is:

"However men may wrong you, do not return an evil.

Do not judge or go to law."

Commandment Five: Love without Fail

Jesus: You have heard that commanded you to love your neighbor, and hate your enemy. But I tell you that to enter in, you must love your brethren of other Kingdoms as well as your own. Bid well of those who hate you, attack you, and willfully cause you harm. Speak and do good to others regardless of how they treat you. Love without regard for the unjust conditions of this world.

Treat all creatures equally well regardless of their differences and live as sons and daughters of the Kingdom of God.

"To me God is truth and love, God is ethics and morality, God is fearlessness."   –Gandhi

My love of nationalism is that my country may become free, that if need be the whole of the country may die so that the human race may live.   –Gandhi

And so this is the fifth commandment:

"Love all people equally well. There are no separate nations in the Kingdom of God."

And so:

1. Do not anger or offend, make peace with all people.

2. Do not lust, threaten or fear abandonment.

3. Do not promise anything on oath to anyone.

4. Do not do not return an evil, do not judge or go to law.

5. Love all people without distinction.

All these commandments may be joined in one:

"Do unto others as you would do unto yourself."

Do not fulfill these commandments for the praises of Men. When you do good to others, do not boast. That is what the commercial religioniests do to obtain the admiration of men. But I tell you, they have their reward. But when you do good to men, do it so that no one sees it, and that your left hand should not know what your right hand does. What is done in the spirit of the Kingdom is in itself, more than sufficient reward.

When You Pray

Jesus: If you wish to pray, don't do as the hypocrites have taught you. They love to pray in the churches and in the sight of men for they seek the glory of Men. And from Men will their reward be due. But if you wish to pray to God, go where no one will see you and then your prayers will be heard. Another thing, don't use vain repetitions when you pray. That's what the hypocrites do. The spirit knows your needs before you even open your lips. Pattern your prayer in this most humble way:

"Our Father which art in heaven, Hallowed be thy name. Thy kingdom come. Thy will be done in earth, as it is in heaven. Give us this day our daily bread. **And forgive us our debts, as we forgive our debtors.** Let us not be led to temptation, but deliver us from evil: For thine is the Kingdom, and the power, and the glory, for ever. Amen."

–Matthew 6:9–13

Benny Hinn making a show of prayer.

Most people miss the significance of Jesus referencing

"debts" in his prayer. We see parallels between financial and emotional debts throughout Jesus' teachings. The key is in recognizing that the source disparity is from within rather than without. The feeling of being slighted has more to do with our own inflated or faltering ego than anything someone may have done to us. Jesus reminded us that with our own imperfect minds, were are incapable of judging the character or intentions of our "debtors." We should pray to be free from taking offense or harboring malice against another. The light of the Kingdom will come from within the hearts and minds of Man.

"Let us forgive each other – only then will we live in peace"

–Leo Tolstoy

The weak can never forgive. Forgiveness is the attribute of the strong.

–Mahatma Gandhi

Darkness cannot drive out darkness; only light can do that. Hate cannot drive out hate; only love can do that.

–Martin Luther King, Jr.

Forgiveness does not mean condoning what has been done. Forgiving means abandoning your right to pay back the perpetrator in his own coin.

– Desmond Tutu

If you Fast

Jesus: If you fast, ensure that it is in a natural manifestation of bereavement rather than the appearance of it. Be not as the hypocrites for they disfigure their faces with wretched expressions so that they may appear to grieve. Verily I say unto you, they have their reward. If you desire to fast, do so in solemn sorrow. Anoint your head, and wash your face so as not to put on airs before Men.

The photo below, titled "Jesus among the Doctors" (Albrecht Dürer, 1506) depicts a twelve year old Jesus debating with six learned scribes at Solomon's Temple in Jerusalem. Their emaciated faces is indicative of fasting. It is based on a passage in Luke. 2:41-52 Notice also, the cryptic hand gestures.

(Thyssen-Bornemisza Museum)

Orthodox Christianity is shrouded in mysticism which ironically, is against everything Jesus stood for. Jesus said, "I have spoken openly to the world, "I always taught in synagogues or at the temple, where all the Jews come together. I said nothing in secret." John 18:20 Only the most naïve of individuals would rather indulge in craven fantasy over cold hard truth.

To Be Rather than to Seem

In pre-Christian India and Ireland (500-700 BC), fasting was used to protest perceived injustices. Such hunger strikes were often carried out right on the front doors of the offenders. It is a widely held misconception that Gandhi partook in a 116 day fast which resulted in the British authorities yielding to his demands. In truth, it was Bhagat Singh who initiated this famous 116 day hunger strike in protest of the abusive treatment of political prisoners. Singh was serving time for the bombing of the Central Legislative Assembly and later hanged for the murder of a British police officer in retribution for the wrongful death of an Indian civilian. He is highly regarded as an Indian revolutionary who prompted India's youth to begin fighting for Indian independence.

Honored with an oversize bronze statue in the Parliament of India, Singh represents the antithesis of

Satyagrahi. Gandhi did participate in several hunger protests, though his longest fast lasted only 21 days. Medical science tells us that the body begins mining muscles and vital organs for energy after this period of time. The loss of bone marrow is an especially dire concern. People have died after only 52 days. How then, did Bhagat Singh survive 116 days? You be the judge.

Wealth & Status vs. the Kingdom

Jesus: Do not lay up for yourselves treasures upon the earth, where moth and rust corrupt, and where thieves break through and steal. Gather up for yourselves treasures in heaven, where neither moth nor rust corrupt, and where thieves do not break through nor steal. For where your treasure is, there will your heart be also. The light of the body is the eye: if therefore your eye be single, your whole body will be full of light. But if your eye be evil, your whole body will be full of darkness.

If the light within you should grow dark, how much darker will this world be? No Man can serve two masters at the same time: in pleasing one, he will offend the other. You cannot serve both God and the flesh. Take no thought for your life, what ye will eat, or what ye will drink; not even for your body any more than your clothing. Is life not more than mere meat, and the body than clothing?

Striving for Self

Jesus Continues: Behold the fowls of the air; for they do not sow, neither do they reap, nor gather into barns; yet God provides them nourishment. Are you worth less than they? Which of you by striving can add the length of your forearm to your height? Then why do you worry about your appearance? Consider the lilies of the field, how they grow. They do not toil, neither do they spin; And yet I say unto you, that even Solomon in all his glory was not arrayed like one of these. Wherefore, if God so clothe the grass of the field, will He not clothe you also? Are you of so little faith?

"Therefore do not think; "What will we eat?" or "What will we drink?" or "How will be will we be clothed?" These are the concerns of the nonbeliever. God knows that ye have need of all these things. Seek first the kingdom of God, and his righteousness; and the material things will be provided to you. Take therefore no thought for tomorrow. Tomorrow will take care of itself. Today has more than its fair share of problems."

Jesus continues: Ask, and it shall be given to you. Seek and you shall find. Knock, and it shall be opened to you.

For every one that asks, receives; those that seek, find; and to whoever knock, it shall be opened. If a child shall ask for food of any of you that is a parent, will you give him a stone? If he ask for nourishment, will you give him poison? I you then, being imperfect, understand the value of giving good gifts to your children how much more shall your creator give to them that ask?

"Feed My Starving Children," a nonprofit Christian organization feeding children in the Philippines.

Jesus told his followers to give without concern for tomorrow. The birds do not sow; neither do they reap and gather into the barns. Yet God provides them with nourishment. Jesus tells us to consider the lilies of the field. They do not toil, neither do they spin. And yet even Solomon in all his glory was not arrayed like even one of them. Those of rational mind would say, "But what of the starving children, not only in third world countries, but right here in the United States?" If "God knows what we need," why does He allow a child starve to death every 10 seconds?

Maybe it's time to change the way we define "God."

Allegory of the Long Spoons

A man who had died and brought back to life was asked, "What was it like?" The man said, "Well I found myself in room filled with hungry souls. They were standing around a large pot of mouthwatering soup. They each held a spoon with exaggeratedly long handles which made it impossible feed themselves. The sight was insufferable! I called out to God for help but nothing happened. Suddenly, I plunged my oversized spoon in the stew and began feeding the ravenous figures from the other side of the pot. I worried that I might not feed them in time. But then, a funny thing happened. They began to feed each other! Right before my very eyes, they were transformed from total strangers to dear departed loved ones. We laughed and we cried. Love and mercy makes a world of difference.

The allegory of the Long Spoons demonstrates the importance of perception in determining one's ultimate reality. But to advance the Kingdom of Heaven on earth, will require much more than a solitary act of faith. Jesus said that to do all is required, we must go and sell all that we have and give to the poor. We know that Gandhi did this, and that he changed the world in the process. But there are others...

"Walked Her Talk."

In 1952 Mildred Lisette Norman became the first woman to walk the entire length of the Appalachian Trail in one season. Then on January 1, 1953, she relinquished all her possessions (including her name) and began a pilgrimage crossing the United States more than 8 times on foot. What was her message?

"This is the way of peace: overcome evil with good, and falsehood with truth, and hatred with love."

During her 28 year cross-country trek (she called optimistic hiking) Peace would talk to people about her philosophy of peace, both within and without. She accepted no gifts, monetary or otherwise and never asked anyone for anything. Peace went without food or shelter unless offered to her. Yet her needs were always met.

"I seldom miss more than four meals in a row"

For the final three decades of her life, Peace wore the same outfit, with segments being repaired or replaced by friends she met along the way.

"I was determined to live at the need level, that is, I didn't want more than I need when so many have less than they need."

Peace revealed very little of her life prior to the pilgrimage. Few people knew of her age, where she grew up or even her birth name. Once, she was asked the purpose of her exceeding modesty...

"I would much rather they remember the important things instead of the very unimportant things."

The "important thing" for Peace was (for lack of a better word) peace. Like Jesus, she propagate the seeds of the Kingdom everywhere she went. Only she wasn't religious. Peace grew up in a modest but supportive and secular household.

"I had a very favorable beginning, although many of you might not think so. I was born poor on a small farm on the outskirts of a small town, and I'm thankful for that. I was happy in my childhood. I had a woods to play in and a creek to swim in and room to grow. I wish that every child could have growing space because I think children are a little like plants. If they grow too close together they become thin and sickly and never obtain maximum growth. We need room to grow."

As a child, Peace thrived in such an environment. She was reciting lengthy poems at age three and learned to read at age the four or five. She taught herself to play the piano in one summer and at age 16, had the highest grade average in her SENIOR class.

(Whittier Transcript, 1979, p.41) According to those closest to her, young Mildred was a far cry from the Pilgrim of peace she would become. The following is an excerpt from what Eugene Young, Peace Pilgrim's brother-in-law had to say...

"The ascension to the role of Peace Pilgrim is all the more astounding. While Mildred's background was intellectual and moral, there was little evidence of the

altruistic, self-sacrificing traits so prominent in the personality of Peace Pilgrim. In order for her to become Peace Pilgrim, it was necessary for her to undergo a complete revision. This goes far to explain why so many of her family and former friends actually rejected her. She was no longer the Mildred they knew and therefore beyond their comprehension!"

The first time Peace graced the inside of a church was at the age of 16 to attend a wedding. Considered by many as a "modern mystic," Peace didn't believe in irrational explanations. What she did believe in however, was God...

"Of course I love everyone I meet. How could I fail to? Within everyone is the spark of God. I am not concerned with racial or ethnic background or the color of one's skin; all people look to me like shining lights!"

What brought on this gradual process awakening? It all began with a simple refusal of indifference...

"I became increasingly uncomfortable about having so much while my brothers and sisters were starving. Finally, I had to find another way. The turning point came when, in desperation and out of a very deep seeking for a meaningful way of life, I walked all one night through the woods. I came to a moonlight glade and prayed. I felt a complete willingness, without reservations, to give my life—to dedicate my life—to service.  "Please use me!" I prayed to God. And a great peace came over me."

For 15 years, Peace struggled between what she called the "lower and higher" self...

"The body, mind and emotions are instruments which can be used by either the self-centered nature or the God-centered nature. The self-centered nature uses these instruments, yet it is never fully able to control them, so there is a constant struggle. They can only be fully controlled by the God-centered nature. When the God-centered nature takes over, you have found inner peace.... The self-centered nature is a very formidable enemy and it struggles fiercely to retain its identity. It defends itself in a cunning manner and should not be regarded lightly. It knows the weakest spots in your armor...During these periods of attack, maintain a humble stature and be intimate with none but the guiding whisper of your higher self."

In his memoire, "From Yeravda Mandir: Ashram Observations" Gandhi describes a similar insight:

"Needless to say, this is not a plea for inertia. Every moment of our life should be filled with mental or physical activity, but that activity should be sattvika, tending to truth. One who has consecrated his life to service learn to distinguish between good activity and evil activity. This discernment goes naturally with a single-minded devotion to service."

Peace wanted to share her newfound elation with the world. Wherever she went, she shared the following steps to inner and outer peace with whoever would listen:

There are four purifications:

1. of body
2. of thoughts
3. of desires
4. of motivations

There are four relinquishments:

1. of self-will
2. of the feeling of separateness
3. of all attachments
4. of all negative feelings

There are four preparations:

1. right attitude toward life.
2. bringing our lives into harmony with the laws that govern this universe.
3. finding one's special place in the universe through inner guidance.
4. simplification of life.

These steps "are not to be taken in any certain order", Peace would say. The first for one person may not be the same for another.

Gandhi himself struggled with giving up his possessions. But he realized that the only way to remain unscathed "by untruth... by what is known as political gain" is total relinquishment...

"... it was a difficult struggle in the beginning and it was wrestle with my wife and–as I can vividly recall–with my children also. But be that as it may, I came definitely to the conclusion that, if I had to serve the people in whose midst my life was cast and of whose difficulties I was a witness from day to day, I must discard all wealth, all possession.... I cannot tell you with truth that, when this belief came to me, I discarded everything immediately. I must confess to you that progress at first was slow. And now, as I recall those days of struggle, I remember that it was also painful in the beginning. But, as days went by, I saw that I had to throw overboard many other things which I used to consider as mine, and a time came when it became a matter of positive joy to give up those things. And one after another, then, by almost geometric progression, the things slipped away from me… And, as I am describing my experiences, I can say a great burden fell off my shoulders, and I felt that I could now walk with ease and do my work also in the service of my fellow–men with great comfort and still greater joy. The possession of anything then became a troublesome thing and a burden."

Gandhi continues: Exploring the cause of that joy, I found that, If I kept anything as my own, I had to defend it against the whole world. I found also that there were many people who did not have the thing, although they wanted it; and I would have to seek police assistance also if hungry, famine-stricken people, finding me in a lonely place, wanted not merely to divide the thing with me but to dispossess me. And I said to myself, if they want it and would take it, they do so not from any malicious motive, but they would do it because theirs was a greater need than mine.

"It is open to the world...to laugh at my dispossessing myself of all property. For me the dispossession has been a positive gain. I would like people to compete with me in my contentment. It is the richest treasure I own. Hence it is perhaps right to say that, though I preach poverty, I am a rich man!"

Peace would say, "... just take whatever steps seem easiest for you and as you take a few steps it will become easier to take a few more." Relinquishment, though difficult, seems to be the key...

"The path of gradual relinquishment...is a difficult path, for only when relinquishment is complete do the rewards really come. The path of quick relinquishments is an easy path, for it brings immediate blessings."

A 1964 radio broadcast in which Peace discussed in the steps detail, has been transcribed in a booklet titled "Steps Toward Inner Peace." The booklet has  been distributed throughout world free of charge (courtesy of her friends) been along with the "Peace Pilgrim" book. On the cover of the book is a picture of Peace in her later years, contently walking down a stretch of highway. Once, she was asked for a convenient time that she might join another in prayer from across a distance. She indicated that because she practiced "ceaseless prayer" they could just pick any time at random and join her. It was while walking, that Peace experienced the initial stages of her awakening. Peace described it as thus...

"...I was out walking in the early morning. All of a sudden I felt very uplifted, more uplifted than I had ever been. I remember I knew timelessness and spacelessness and lightness. I did not seem to be walking on the earth. There were no people, or even animal around, but every flower, every bush, every tree seemed to wear a halo. There was a light emanation around everything and flecks of gold fell like slanted rain through the air....The most important part was not the phenomena: the important part of it was the realization of the oneness of all creation."

Matthew 19:27-28 records that Peter asked Jesus what the reward will be for having forsaken all their possessions and following him. Jesus supposedly said that "in the regeneration, when the Son of man shall sit in the throne of his glory, ye also shall sit upon twelve thrones, judging the twelve tribes of Israel..." This obvious plagiary doesn't not sit well with the astute reader. For in Matthew 19:29-30 Jesus says that the in the Kingdom it is the meek that are exalted...

"And every one that hath forsaken houses, or brethren, or sisters, or father, or mother, or wife, or children, or lands, for my name's sake, shall receive an hundredfold, and shall inherit everlasting life. But many that are first shall be last; and the last shall be first."

Unlike Gandhi, Mildred Ryder never compiled a manuscript. Much of what we know about her spiritual transformation was gathered from letters and informal conversations between Peace and her friends. John and Ann Rush recorded and transcribed some of them (accessible from peacepilgrim.com). A very encouraging snippet from one of those conversations concerns the struggle between the values of this world and the Kingdom...

John: "When you began your struggles, did it seen rather hopeless to you? very difficult? that you would never attain this...maturity?"

Ann: "Or did you know what you were seeking?"

Peace: "I... You see I didn't really know what was happening to me except that my life was improving. Now, when I went through that struggle – after all, I was used to the valleys, I had been in them constantly before – I said 'Now there are some hilltops!

"Isn't this wonderful! Life is improving! There are some hilltops now."

John Rush: "But when you went back into the valleys you weren't depressed?"

Peace: "No, because I always had the feeling eventually I would come back again on the hilltop. I have always been able to accept myself and the experiences I was going through very easily as being perfectly natural. What I concentrated on was my cause.

You may have noticed quite a few pages have been dedicated to Peace Pilgrim (in this book as well as the website). Along with Gandhi, she is one of the few recently documented examples of Jesus' life and teachings. Again, the interesting thing about Peace is that she didn't read the Gospels until after she had already relinquished her old life and began her three decade crusade for peace! Interestingly, she credits the same source that Jesus did.* Peace did eventually read the Gospels for the sake of the Christians she so often encountered along her journey. Her life of selfless servitude, is a testament to the secular teachings of Christianity.

*John 3:32-34, 5:19, 6:38-40, 7:16, 7:28-29, 8:28, 8:38, 8:40, 12:49, 17:8

"Though really dedicated people can offset the ill effects of masses of out-of-harmony people, so we who work for peace must not falter."

–Peace Pilgrim

One reporter in a Texas newspaper, said fondly of Mildred: "She literally brought heaven onto earth. She brought the divine qualities into her life here...She changed lives all over America." People like Mildred

Ryder, Tolstoy, Gandhi, MLK and Nelson Mandela motivate us to strive for perfection. But Jesus told us that to reach this state of perfections, we must first go and sell everything we own and give to the poor.

Gandhi. Why should all of us possess property? Why should not we, after a certain time, dispossess ourselves of all property? Unscrupulous merchants do this for dishonest purpose. Why may we not do it for a moral and a great purpose? For a Hindu it was the usual thing at a certain stage. Every good Hindu is expected, after having lived the household life for a certain period, to enter upon a life of non-possession of property. Why may we not revive the noble tradition? In effect it merely amounts to this that for maintenance we place ourselves at the mercy of those to whom we transfer our property.

Gandhi Continues. To me the idea is attractive. In the innumerable cases of such honourable trust there is hardly one case in a million of abuse of trust. .How such a practice can be worked without giving handle to dishonest persons can only be determined after long experimenting. No one, however, need be deterred from trying the experiment for fear of the example being abused. The divine author of Gita was not deterred from delivering the message of he 'Song Celestial' although he probably knew that it would be tortured to justify every variety of vice including murder.

Finding Your Way

Jesus taught that to receive life, we must be "born of the Spirit." With imperfect minds that is, we must relinquish those things which cause us to compare ourselves with one another by the inequitable measures of this unjust world. Rather, we must remain faithful to the still voice within. Those who follow the whims of the flesh, are as lemurs following one another over a cliff. Until we break away from the foal and are born of the Spirit, we will not enter the Kingdom of God.

Jesus: Wide is the gate and broad is the way that leads to ruin for that is the path that most people take. Strait is the path, and narrow is the way, that leads unto true life, because few are those that find it.

Discerning the Wolves

Jesus: Beware of false prophets, which come to you in sheep's clothing. Inwardly they are but ravening wolves. But they can be identified by their fruits. Do men gather grapes of thorns, or figs of thistles? Even so every good tree bringeth forth good fruit; but a corrupt tree bringeth forth evil fruit. A good tree cannot bring forth evil fruit, neither can a corrupt tree bring forth good fruit. Every tree that fails to bring forth good fruit is cut down, and cast into the fire. In a like manner you will divide them by their fruits. Not every person who says "Lord, Lord" shall enter into the Kingdom of Heaven. Only those who are sincere will enter in. Many will claim to prophesize, cast out devils, and perform many wonderful works in the name of God? But these workers of iniquity will be found out and divided. Whosoever receives the Kingdom teachings and abides by them is like a wise man who builds his house upon a rock. When the rain fell, the floods came and the winds blew and beat upon that house. But it did not fall for its foundation was build upon that rock. But for every one that receives the teachings and does not honor them is like a foolish man who built his house upon the sand. When the floods came and the winds blew and beat upon that house… it fell. The damage done to that house was great.

The people were astonished with Jesus' teachings for he taught them with a depth of understanding unlike that of the scribes. Then Jesus rejoiced saying...

Jesus. I thank the O God, the source of all things in heaven and earth, who has revealed what was hidden from the wise and learned to the simple, because they acknowledge themselves as children of the Kingdom. ... Blessed are your eyes and ears. For I tell you, that many prophets and kings have desired to see those things which you have seen and to hear those things which you have heard here today. And yet they neither saw nor did they hear them. All who concern themselves for their own wellbeing have put on a yoke not meant for them to bear. Come unto me, all ye that labor and are heavy laden, and I will give you rest. Take my yoke upon you, and learn of me; for I am meek and lowly in heart. If you abide by my teachings, you will find rest unto your souls. For my yoke is easy, and my burden is light.

Rational Jesus

Sometime after this, Jesus went up to Jerusalem for the feast of the Jews. There was a pond there by the sheep market which was said to have been frequented by an Angel. This was supposedly evidenced by the stirring of water within the pool. Whoever was first to step into the "troubling of the water" was thought to be healed of whatever ailed them. Jesus saw a man who had been lying there for a long time.

Jesus: You have yet to be made whole?"

The feeble man: Sir, I have no one to assist me into the pool. After the water stirs, another steps down in front of me.

Jesus: take up thy bed, and leave this superstitious place.

Religionist bystanders: But it is the Sabbath day. It is unlawful for you to carry your bedding?"

After some time, the elderly man identified Jesus as the one who had "caused the stir" and the commercial religionists were glad to finally have "just" cause against him. Remember, Mosaic Law prescribed the death penalty for the breaking of the Sabbath. It is hopeful that our current penal system will one day be looked upon with a similar disgust as does this.

Jesus to the Religionists: "I am guided by the Spirit of God within me rather than the traditions of Man.

Jesus had not only broken the Sabbath, but claimed to be one with God. After this, the religionist sought even harder to impose the death penalty upon him. Jesus did not falter. Rather, he stood among the spectators and called for the children of the Kingdom to action...

Jesus: A child of the Kingdom does nothing to glorify himself but is obedient to the spirit. These little things that seem radical to you now are only a sample of what needs to be done. Those of you that hear the voice of the Spirit experienced but a hint of its liberating power. Those who answer the call have more than a mere glimpse of the Kingdom; they transition from purgatory unto life. I tell you, the time has arrived for those lying in slumber to arise and take up the mantle. The children of the Kingdom have the authority of understanding. Marvel not at this, for the time has come for those lying in wake to hear God's voice and arise. The reward for abiding by the Spirit is life: that which is illusory for those who do not. I am not at the mercy of my flesh because I am obedient to the Spirit. As such, my judgment is just. As for my accusers, I could vouch for the sincerity of my actions but they would just as easily invalidate it.

Jesus continues: There is another that came forward in witness of me whose virtue is in your high esteem. Yes, they sent of John, and he bare witness unto the truth. But understand that I do not require testimony from any man. These things that I say and do are not in resistance of those who would take my life but so that you might receive it. You accepted John and for a while regarded him highly. But I produce a greater witness than that of John. For the works which have been entrusted to me, these very works for which I stand accused bear sufficient proof that I am a servant of God. But you have neither heard the voice of the Spirit at any time, nor seen even a glimpse of the Kingdom. You could not accept even John's testimony for whom you sent because you do not have God's word abiding in you. Search your scriptures for which you believe hold the key to eternal life. They also provide sufficient testimony, yet you still will not accept my teachings and receive life. I do not seek the glory of Men for that which is not bequeathed of God. is worth nothing. My teachings are directly from the Spirit but you cannot identify it, so you will not accept me. But if another should come under his own endorsement, him you would receive.

Jesus continues: How can Men believe, who seek glory from one another rather than the honor that cometh only from God? Do not think that I wish to convince you even by your own teachings. For had you truly believed in them, you would know the value of mine. If you don't believe in the veracity even of your own words, how shall ye believe anyone else's?

More Shall Be Given

Jesus. For the kingdom of heaven is as a man preparing to venture into a foreign land. He called his servants, and delivered unto them his wealth. To the first, he gave the value of five. To the second, he gave two. And to the third, he gave one. To each of them he gave relative to his ability and immediately he went away. The servant who had received the five talents went and traded with them and yielded five more. Similarly, the servant who had received two earned from them four. But the one that had received the least went and buried within the earth that which he had been trusted. After a period of time, the lord returned and called for a reckoning. He that had received five units came and brought forth ten saying, "Lord, you entrusted me with five units. Behold, I have gained five more. To this the lord replied, "Well done, you are a good and faithful servant. Because you have been faithful over a few things, I will make you ruler over many. Join with me in celebration. The servant who had received two talents then came forth saying, "Lord, you entrusted me with two units. Behold, I have gained two additional. Again, the lord replied, "Well done, you are a good and faithful servant. Because you have been faithful over a few things, I will make you ruler over many. Join with me in celebration. Then the servant whom had been entrusted only one portion came forth saying, "Lord, I knew that you are a hard man, reaping where you have not sown, and gathering where you have not laid straw. Because of this, I was afraid. I went and hid the endowment in the dirt. Thus, I have preserved what you have entrusted me. To this, the lord proclaimed, "You are a trifling and lazy servant, you say that I reap where I have not sown, and gather where I have not laid straw. If so, you should have left my money to the exchangers, and then at my coming I should have received my advance plus interest. Take from him all that was trusted, and give it to the one that has ten."

Jesus summaries the moral of the parable:

"To everyone that makes good use of all that has been entrusted, more shall be given in abundance.

But from those that give less, more shall be taken away."

Those who readily receive guidance from the Spirit can be likened to a good steward. Because they sow the seeds of the Kingdom, more is entrusted to them. Conversely, there are those that dim their light for fear of diminished social standing. Those that are ashamed, doubtful or afraid are like the trite and slothful servant who lost what little vision they safeguarded within themselves. Because such a person so values the illusory and unjust ways of this realm, they unwittingly forfeit their heavenly birthright. One cannot serve two masters.

Those That Have

-Mark[12:41-44] records that Jesus once sat in the temple watching as people gave their offerings. He noticed that many of the wealthy people gave a lot of money but then a poor widow came and put in only two coins. Jesus then called his disciples over and commented that the poor widow had put in more than all the others. Though the others gave what they thought would be socially acceptable, this poor woman gave all that she had. This story compliments the parable in Matthew [20:1-16] where the workers in the vineyard who had labored all day in the hot sun felt superior to those who arrived later in the day. Yet they received the same pay as those who had worked only a few hours. (See also, pg. 240)

One should never use a perceived inadequacy as an excuse for inaction. Neither should we let intimidation or a feeling of incompetence hinder us from talking to people about the true message of Jesus' life and teachings, animal rights or global warming. Maybe they speak eloquently, recite bible verses verbatim or are otherwise domineering. No person should ever be denied the Kingdom based on their level of sophistication or lack thereof. Jesus told his disciples to share the gospel (good news) with everyone who will listen and to shake the dust off their feet as a testimony against whoever refuses to hear the truth. The relative size of our contribution matters little in comparison to the effort we expend.

One True Miracle

Jesus sent his disciples to spread the doctrine of the Kingdom. For their journey, they were to carry nothing but the clothes on their back. No cane to fend off wild animals, no food, no pouch and no money. They weren't to wonder from one place to another, but to stay in whatever house they were welcomed into and deliver the house from there. When the apostles returned, Jesus took them on private leave to a deserted place in Bethsaida to recuperate and discuss their pilgrimages. They were obviously in great need of leave. But when their location became known, the people came and Jesus received them warmly ministering to them about the Kingdom and consoling the weary.

Near the end of the day, the disciples pleaded for Jesus to send the crowd back into the towns to seek food and lodging. Jesus said simply, "Give them something to eat." The disciples responded, "We have only five loaves and two fishes. Should we should go and buy food for 5000 people? Jesus said to them, "Make them sit down in groups of 50." Looking up to sky, Jesus blessed the bread, broke it and placed it into 12 baskets. The disciples divided the bread into smaller portions and dispersed it into the groups who shared amongst themselves what little they were given. Soon the spirit came over them. Those that brought rations began to give to those that had none. They ate in this way until all were filled with food left over.

Note: To suppose that 5000 would venture into the deserted area without food is almost as absurd as believing that Jesus would neglect the perfect opportunity to illustrate the feasibility of the Kingdom philosophy. Pulling bread out of thin air validates nothing more than self-aggrandizement?

"A child of the Kingdom does nothing to glorify himself but is obedient to the spirit."

In reference to bread, miracle working and desolate places, this passage is reminiscent of Jesus' fast in the wilderness. Overwhelmed with hunger, Jesus finds himself confronted with the spirit of doubt,

Spirit of Doubt: If you were truly a child of God, you could command these stones to turn into bread."

Jesus: I live not by bread alone, but by the will of God which is far greater than the will of my flesh.

The religionist would have you believe that Jesus had made bread from thin air as "Moses had done in the wilderness." But Jesus' ministry extolled the total relinquishment of personal possessions which is the ultimate act of faith. He was in the middle of ministering the Kingdom to the crowd which extols the virtue of austereness and selfless love. Why would anyone sell everything they have and give to those that have none? Jesus could just teach them to make magically delicious food from thin air?

Gandhi. Non-possession is allied to non-stealing. A thing not originally stolen must nevertheless be classified as stolen property, if we possess it without needing it. Possession implies provision for the future. A seeker after Truth, a follower of the law of Love, cannot hold anything against tomorrow. God never stores for tomorrow. He never creates more than what is strictly needed for the moment. If, therefore, we repose faith in His Providence, we should rest assured that He will give us every day our daily bread, meaning everything that we require.... Our ignorance or negligence of the Divine Law, which gives to man from day to day his daily bread and no more, has given rise to inequalities with all the miseries attendant upon them. The rich have superfluous store of things which they do not need and which are, therefore, neglected and wasted, while millions are starved to death for want of sustenance... If each retained possession of only what he needed, no one would be in want, and all would live in contentment. As it is, the rich are discontented no less than the poor. The poor man would fain become a millionaire, and the millionaire a multi-millionaire....

Gandhi Continues: The rich should take the initiative in dispossession with a view to a universal diffusion of the spirit of contentment. If only they keep their own property within moderate limits, the starving will be easily fed, and will learn the lesson of contentment along with the rich... Perfect fulfillment of the ideal of non-possession requires that man should, like the birds, have no roof over his head, no clothing and no stock of food for the morrow. He will indeed need his daily bread, but it will be God's business, and not his, to provide it. Only the fewest possible, if any at all, can reach this ideal. We ordinary seekers may not be repelled by the seeming impossibility. But we must keep the ideal constantly in view, and in the light thereof, critically examine our possessions and try to reduce them... Civilization, in the real sense of the term, consists not in the multiplication, but in the deliberate and voluntary reduction of wants. This alone promotes real happiness and contentment, and increases the capacity for service...From the standpoint of pure truth, the body too is a possession. It has been truly said that desire for enjoyment creates bodies for the soul.

Gandhi Continues: When this desire vanishes, there remains no further need for the body, and man is free from the vicious cycle of births and deaths. The soul is omnipresent; why should she care to be confined within the cage-like body, or do evil and even kill for the sake of the cage?... We thus arrive at the ideal of total renunciation, and learn to use the body for the purpose of service so long as it exists, so much so that service and not bread becomes with us the staff of life. We eat and drink, sleep and wake for service alone. Such an attitude of mind brings us real happiness, and the beatific vision in the fullness of time. Let us all examine ourselves from this standpoint...Needless to say, this is not a plea for inertia. Every moment of our life should be filled with mental or physical activity, but that activity should be sattvika, tending to truth. One who has consecrated his life to service learn to distinguish between good activity and evil activity. This discernment goes naturally with a single-minded devotion to service.

Again, If Jesus had been performing miracles left and right, why would his disciples interrupt his teachings and plead for him to send the crowd back to town for food and lodging? Furthermore, why would he himself ask what food they had? He needed what little they had to seed a miracle.

It makes much more sense that Jesus would use the scarcity of food to illustrate the Kingdom teachings. Jesus and his disciples gave what little food they had to those that had none? He planted the seeds, and the Kingdom emerged. The people who brought food gave to those who had none until all were fed with some left over! Our true sustenance for life is not bread, but to serve a purpose greater than our own. Jesus and his disciples went into the wilderness to rest. They sought peace and solitude. The easy way out, would have been to send the people back to the city. But for Jesus, nothing meant more than his ministry. When the crowd dispersed, Jesus sought solitude once more. But the people found him the following day. Again, he welcomes them warmly. In one day's time, they had already forgotten the miracle of 5000 fed and sought even more proof that his message was ordained by God...

Jesus: You came in search of miracles but found the one thing you truly desired most. Do not labor for the food that perishes but for that which nourishes the spirit forever.

The people's preoccupation with miracles caused them to miss the inherent value of the Kingdom teachings. Jesus' austere lifestyle was contrary to that of the Mosaic teachers of Law who dressed in the finest robes and slept near stately palaces. His response indicates that people in the crowd referenced the bread that fell from heaven to feed their forefathers in the wilderness...

Jesus: You had your sign, yet you still do not believe. You ate of the loaves and all were filled. Just as your fathers once ate of manna in the wilderness, yet they are now dead. Those that eat of the bread of life shall live forever.

Note: There are two types of faith addressed by this passage: "mystical faith" and "rational faith." The former variety is based on hope (without decisive action) and is of pagan derivative, having to do with the concept of "mana" or divine power. Many anthropologists (Marrett, R.R. 1909) believe that religion evolved from the idea that certain people possess different levels of this immortal mana. (Mauss et al., 1972) Spiritual teachers were expected to demonstrate mystical abilities. Their followers merely prayed for a miracle and wished for the best. Perhaps a word of caution for the aspiring sage is in order. "Mana" was traditionally transferred through certain ritualistic practices. Namely the sacrificial offering (barbequed) of an innocent consumed in the honor of said deity.

The obvious moral of the story is that a profit shouldn't seem too perfect for the job. Mainstream religionists honor til this day, the primeval assertion that the attainment of eternal life requires the eating of the symbolic flesh of Jesus. Oh, and the drinking of his sacrificial blood

---

After this, Jesus collected another seventy men from among the crowd and sent them (in pairs) on further pilgrimages to places he himself wished to go. Then he addressed them...

Jesus: The harvest is truly great, but the laborers are few. So we should pray to the Lord of the harvest, for him to send more laborers. Begin your ministry right away but be aware that I send you forth as lambs among wolves. Carry nothing: no purse, nor sack of bread. Wear no shoes and salute no man along the way. When you first enter a house, bless it in this way: "Peace be to this house." If the son of peace be there, you will receive rest. Remain there eating and drinking whatever they provide for a laborer is worthy of his hire. Do not wander from house to house. Say to them that listen, "The Kingdom of God is upon (within and without) you." But wherever you are rejected, shake it off and move on. He that receives you, receives me. He that despises you, despises me and he that despises me; despises Him that sent me.

Jesus Responds to Accusers

Not long after this, a crowd of people gathered around a house near Jerusalem where Jesus had been ministering. Religionist professors of the law began to address the crowds in an attempt to discredit the Kingdom teachings. They said that Jesus was possessed of Beelzebub (Chief among devils) and by that authority, he speaks.

As for his casting out demons...

Jesus: Every kingdom divided against itself is brought to desolation; even a house divided against a house will fall. You say that I cast out lowly spirits through Beelzebub. But I ask you this, if Satan be divided against himself, how shall his kingdom stand? If by Beelzebub I cast out spirits of fear and doubt, on what authority do your sons cast them out? Who then are you to judge? If however I with the finger of God cast them out, it stands to reason that the Kingdom of God is from within."

Note: Evaluate the immense value of the Gospels from a historic psychosocial perspective. The ancients considered physical and mental infirmities (autism, epileptic seizures, etc.) to be the work of dumb and deaf demons. They thought the same of anyone who questioned the teachings of the church.

People brought their children to see Jesus so that they might have these doubtful "demons" cast out. Matthew 12:22, 17:15; Mark 5:23, 7:26, 9:25, 10:13; Luke 9:38, 11:14; John 4:47

The book of Mark 9:17-29 records one such occasion where a man amongst the crowd came forward with his child who obviously suffered from epilepsy.

Parent: Teacher, I have brought you my son who is possessed by a dumb spirit. And wherever it seizes him, it tears at him and he foams and gnashes his teeth and he becomes dehydrated. Moreover, I told your disciples to cast it out, but they couldn't.

Jesus: O unbelieving generation, how long will I be with you? How long will I bear with you? Bring him to me.

The child was brought closer to Jesus. And when the child saw him, the "spirit" immediately convulsed him, and he fell onto the ground, and rolled about, foaming at the mouth.

Jesus: How long has this happened to him?

Father: Since childhood. And it has often thrown him in both fire and water, to destroy him. But if you can do anything, help us and have compassion on us.

Jesus: To them that can believe, everything is possible.

The child's father immediately cried out in tears...

"I believe, Lord. Help my unbelief."

Then when Jesus saw that a crowd was gathering around them, he rebuked the unclean spirit...

Jesus: You dumb and deaf spirit, I command you, come out of him and do not go in to him ever again!

After this, the child shouted and began severely convulsing. Suddenly the child laid still "<u>as one dead; insomuch that many said, He is dead</u>."(Mark 9:26 KJV) But Jesus took hold of his "hand and <u>lifted him up</u>; and he arose" (Benny Hinn Theatrics?). Then when he had gone home, his disciples asked him privately, "Why is it that we could not cast it out?" And he said to them, "This kind (of faith) cannot come out by any means except prayer and fasting" (Mark 9:29). It is doubtful that Jesus, would have played the oncoming crowd in such a way. As for the fasting, he probably would have said that "<u>fasting comes as a result of faith and mourning, not as a consequence of it</u>. But if you must fast, be sure it's not for show." Other NT passages actually record that neither Jesus nor his disciples fasted Matthew 9:14-9:15; Mark 2:18-20; Luke 5:33-35 commercial religion not only stunts spiritual health in that it satiates the natural longing for truth, it keeps people from seeking physical and mental treatment. Many preventable deaths <u>and suicides</u> would have been averted if not for church-house witch-doctors.

Philosophy of Nonresistance

Jesus: When a strong man keeps his palace armed, his goods are secured. But when a man even stronger he should happen upon him… he will take as spoils, all the armor where the former has placed his trust.

Note: In this way, Jesus seizes the opportunity to address both his accusers and halfhearted followers simultaneously. The darkness cannot withstand the light. One must decide once and for all whether to live by might or by that what is eternally right. The path most have chosen is to follow the fleeting adorations of Man wherever it may lead. To choose the authentic life however, is to narrow ones focus, desiring only to usher the coming of the Kingdom with one mind and one accord.

As for the Working of Miracles

Still unsure, the people ask again for Jesus to show them a miracle as a sign of his authority. But those who ask for signs do not acknowledge them for long. Privy to the ploy of those who seek miracles, Jesus calls for a reckoning…

Jesus: He that is not with me is against me and he that does not gather with me scatters about.

As for Indecision

The bystanders obviously felt intimidated by the religionist professors of the law who heckled Jesus. Similarly, many people have seen a glimpse of the Kingdom but their vision has grown dim to the fears and illusory bribes of this world. They know that the gospel, as it is taught is void of meaning and purpose, but they do not dare confront the commercial religionists. Jesus exercised authority over the written word and he did it wherever people gathered, including the churches and the synagogues. We must be careful however, neither to be ashamed nor proud of our beautiful thoughts and aspirations. The more we are given, the greater our thirst. Until we fan that spark within us however, nothing more will be forthcoming. Sadly, most of us shamefully hide our light under a bushel and extinguish the flame. Jesus offers parable after parable on the importance of persistent action, focus and consistency:

THE PRODIGAL SON, Luke 15.11-32;

THE GOOD SAMARITAN, Luke 10.25-37;

THE WORKERS IN THE VINEYARD, Matthew 20.1-16;

THE FRIEND AT MIDNIGHT, Luke 11.5-8;

THE UNFORGIVING SLAVE, Matthew 18.23-35;

THE GREAT BANQUET, Luke 14. 16-24;

THE PHARISEE AND THE TAX COLLECTOR, Luke 18:10-14;

THE UNJUST JUDGE, Luke 18: 2-8;

THE TALENTS, Matthew 25:14-30;

THE UNJUST MANAGER, LUKE 16:1-8

THE RICH MAN AND LAZARUS, Luke 16:19-31

THE FAITHFUL AND WISE SLAVE: Matthew 24:45-51

Luke 12:42-46

THE PARABLE OF THE SOWER, Mark 4:3-8; Matthew 13: 3-
8, Luke 8:5-8

THE RICH FOOL, Luke 12:16-21

THE WEDDING FEAST, Matthew 22: 1-14

THE FINAL JUDGEMENT, Matthew 25:31-46

THE FATHER'S GOOD GIFTS, Matt 7:9-11, Luke 11:11-13

THE TWO SONS, Matthew 21:28-32

THE LOST SHEEP, Luke 15:4-7

THE PARABLE OF THE LEAVEN, Matthew 13:33

THE PARABLE OF THE MUSTARD SEED, Mark 4:30-32
      (See also: Matthew 13:31-32, Luke 13:18-19, Thomas 20)

THE TREASURE IN THE FIELD, Matthew 13:44

THE PEARL OF GREAT PRICE, Matthew 13:45-46

THE LOST COIN, Luke 15:8-10

THE SLAVE AT DUTY, Luke 17:7-10

THE WAITING SLAVES, Mark 13:34-37 (also see Luke 12:35-
38)

THE WEEDS IN THE WHEAT, Matthew 13:24-30

THE WICKED TENANTS, Mark 12:1-12 (also see Matthew
21:33-46, Luke 20:9-19, Thomas 65-66)

THE BARREN FIG TREE, Luke 13:6-9

THE SEED GROWING SECRETLY, Mark 4:26-29

Jesus goes on to impress upon the crowd, the importance of a single unwavering vision.

Jesus: When the lowly spirit is removed, it walks through deserted places seeking rest. Finding none it decides to return to the dwelling from which it came. And when it returns, finding it swept and pleasantly garnished, it goes and gets seven other spirits even more wicked than himself and they enter in and dwell there also. In the end, the cleansed man is thus worse for wear.

Note: Jesus reminded his followers that they cannot strive for the truth and for status and material wealth at the same time for we will inevitably neglect the one for the other. From a strictly rational perspective, Jesus' philosophy makes perfect sense. Absolute truth is true no matter the desired outcome. It makes no difference whether eternal life (consciousness) literally exists. Knowing the finality of our existence doesn't add value to our lives, it voids all meaning. Doing "the right thing" in hopes that your actions will be rewarded is the wrong kind of faith. Such concern negates not only the intrinsic value of an act but also the expansion of self (See weblink at Rationalbible.com, "Capacity to Love"). We should keep our eyes glued on God in relentless service to advance the Kingdom.

Advancing the Kingdom of Heaven

More times than not, our perceived roles (individual, social and ethical) clash. When this occurs, the most predominant held value trumps all others. It goes without saying that Jesus loved his mother and brothers greatly. But to honor them best, he chose to advance the Kingdom. As he spoke, a woman from the thickening crowd shouted:

"Fortunate is the womb that bare thee, and the breast which thou hast sucked."

But Jesus deflected saying,

"More so fortunate are those that hear the word of the spirit, and abide it."

Sometimes, serving the Kingdom might mean risking the affections of our loved ones. The ultimate labor of love however, is to serve the Kingdom. We must perform our familial obligations but not its every superficial customs lest we grow narrow minded and succumb to its many strains. In this manner, the concerns of the world gradually drive out the voice of the spirit.

Once we recognize the common parent stock from which we are all spring, we realize the basic unity of the human family, and there is no room left for enmities and unhealthy competition.

–Gandhi

We know too well the dim fate of innocent creatures who needlessly suffer and die; not only on factory farms but in our rural neighborhoods. Anyone who was brought up on a small family farm can attest to the horror of slaughter days. The cow is strewn by its hind legs, throat slit and skin torn from her body with her heart still beating. All in the first couple years of her more than 25 year natural born life span. We know that it is wrong to stand idle. But we do nothing to stop genocide because we lack conviction, we are too cowardice to act.

Jesus. No man, when he has a lighted candle hides it in a secret place. He doesn't put it under a bushel. He puts it on a candlestick so that everyone who comes in may receive its light.

Free range dairy cows like Sally (picture below) are among the lucky ones. Like all the other dairy cows however, she must be artificially inseminated to

 stimulate her body to produce milk. Sally bellows like all the others too when her newborn calves are snatched from her tit, typically within a day or so of birth. But the farmer needs "his" milk to sell at the market. Sally still doesn't profitably produce enough for mass consumption on her own though...

For that, Sally's body has been pumped with large amounts of hormones (that's why her back legs are bowed in). Since she now produces up to six times the normal amount of milk, the farmer can extract it several times a day. Sadly however, the electronic milking machines shock her and the incessant torture causes lesions. Sally's udders are swollen and constantly bleed. But the farmer treats the milk to remove much of the pus taste that inevitably seeps in. Of course, that means that even "free-range" dairy cows like Sally will spend the entirety of their lives in an unnatural environment of concrete, mud, feces and swarms of flies. When mother's milk is depleted, the grieving cycle begins again and again until her health declines to the point that it is more profitable for the farmer to bring Sally to slaughter like all the others. Turns out, McDonalds hamburgers don't grow on trees after all. They are cut from the spent bodies of cows like Sally.

Next time you drive by a KFC or a TYSON plant, consider what polite society tolerates: 300 six-to eight-week old chicks are killed EVERY SECOND in the U.S. alone. That's 1,080,000 unnecessary and inhumane deaths per hour! By the end of her very brief lifespan, her legs were no longer able to support the oversized genetically manipulated body you see pictured above. Sadly, this chick was not among the lucky ones whose lungs collapsed in response to the ammonia laden air before slaughter.

On that faithful day, this 6 to 8 week old chick was literally thrown into a crate along with several other oversized baby chicks and shipped to the slaughter house. On arrival, her bowed legs were mechanically slammed onto conveyer belt hooks that dragged her head through electrified water which paralyzed her neck for the blades that cut her throat. With her heart still beating, she was scalded with boiling water for the ease of plucking her feathers from her tormented body.

The piglet you see below represents one of the 24,000 slaughtered each day in the U.S. alone. Within 24 hours of her birth, her ears will be clipped or tattooed, her needle teeth cut and her tail chopped off. Her brothers will be castrated to ensure his body will  produce tender meat. All this will be done by factory workers without the use of anesthetics. She will spend the remaining 5-6 months of her "life" in an iron stall with cement floors and no room to turn or satisfy her inborn urge to burrow. On that faithful day she will finally see the light of day as ship her off to slaughter. The blood-curdling screams of her brothers and sisters are without a doubt among the most horrible sound ever heard. She too will have her throat cut and submerged into boiling water (often fully alive) before limbs are torn from her body all for the sake of Man's yearning of bacon and ham.

For thousands of years, religionists have waxed poetic about virtue but where are the fruits of all their labors? Perhaps it time to pull our heads out of the proverbial sands of self-righteous indignation and relinquish petty indifferences of creed? Devoid the blinders of religion, its naturally conscientious practitioners might actually put an end to the cause of unspeakable murder they now call fellowship meat. Despite the admonitions of its founders, what has now become commercialized religion does nothing but, endorse the otherwise intolerable habits of their parishioners. The religionist can rant til blue in the face about the obvious merits of peace, love and compassion but can she retain her position and hold her tithing payers accountable at the same time?

The Orthodox Church would rather establish insignificant rules (length of hair, dress, etc.) that do little more than separate their members from society rather than to condemn such cruel and mindless amusements such as animal hunting, bull and cock fighting, fishing and horse racing! The hypocrite is even permitted to wear the furs and skins of tortured animals into the church!! Even more shocking, is the consumption of innocent victims of violent deaths at Church sanctioned potluck dinners!!!

Jesus: You blind guides, which strain at a gnat, and swallow a camel. You religionists wash the outside of your cup and platter; but your innermost part is full of ravening and wickedness. Didn't God make the outward part as well as the inward? Make yourself clean through and through.

Why We Hesitate

The shameful truth is that we hesitate to speak for the voiceless for the vague possibility that there is something of greater value at stake for us personally. That is, we hold out for nonexistent honor of Men rather than of God (truth) BECAUSE we foolishly cling to the inequitable treasures of this world and we foolishly assume that greater opportunities for martyrdom will be given. The book of Luke, chapter 14 contains one of Jesus' most powerful calls to action. Jesus was seated at the table of an influential religionist when he was confronted by a professor of Mosaic Law who asked his opinion on whether it was permissible to do good works on the Sabbath.

Jesus: Which of you shall have an ass or an ox fallen into a pit, and will not straightway pull him out on the Sabbath day?

As usual, the religionists were dumbfounded by Jesus rational response. Then, Jesus commented on how the guests had secured for themselves, the most honored places at the table...

Jesus: When a man invites you to a wedding banquet, don't look for the most honored place at his table. For he may hold another man more honorably than you. The host will come to you and say, "Give your place to this other guest" and you will begin with shame to take the lowest place. Rather, when you are invited, go and sit in the worst place in the room. Then, when your host comes, he will say, "My friend, go up higher; then you will have honor in the sight of those sitting with you. For everyone who exalts himself will be humbled, and he who humbles himself will be exalted."

Jesus turned to his host and said, "When you prepare a dinner or a supper, don't invite your friends, nor your brethren. Don't invite your kinsmen nor your rich neighbors in hopes that they might return the favor by inviting you also. Rather, when thou prepare a feast, call for the poor, the maimed, the lame and the blind. ; <u>They cannot recompense you,</u> but you will stand among the just. When one of the guest eating with them acknowledge what he had said, Jesus said "Blessed is he that shall eat bread in the kingdom of God." Then he addressed the man personally...

Jesus: Friend, A certain man made a great supper, and invited many guests. He sent his servant at supper time to say to the invited, "Come; for everything is ready." But each one of them gave an excuse. The first said, "I have bought a piece of ground, and I have to go and see it; I pray thee have me excused. And another said, I have bought five yoke of oxen, and I go to prove them; I pray thee have me excused. And another said, I have married a wife, and therefore I cannot come. So that servant came, and told his lord these things. Then the master of the house (being angry) said to his servant, Go out quickly into the streets and lanes of the city, and bring in hither the poor, and the maimed, and the halt, and the blind. And the servant said, Lord, I have done as you have commanded, and yet there is still room. And the lord said unto the servant, Go out into the highways and hedges and compel them to come in so that my house may be filled. For I tell you now, none of those people who were first invited shall taste of my supper."

Later on, a crowd of people had gathered around Jesus obviously in hopes of receiving personal discipleship. He turned to them and said If anyone comes to him valuing the love of his father, mother, brethren, sisters, wife, child, or even his own life more than true righteousness will not be able to bear the burdens of the Spirit (represented by his carrying of the cross) and as such, cannot be disciple of him.

Jesus: For which of you, intending to build a tower, does not sit down first, and count the cost, to determine if you have sufficient funds to finish it? Lest he find that after having laid the foundation and is not able to finish it, everyone will see what he had done commence to mocking him saying, "This man began to build and was not able to finish." Or what king, going to make war against another king, does not sit down first, and consult on whether he will be able with ten thousand men to meet him that comes against him with twenty thousand? Or else, while the other is still a great way off, he will have to send an ambassador desiring conditions of peace. So likewise, whoever is among you that has not already forsaken all that he has cannot be my disciple. Salt is good. But if the salt have lost his savor, wherewith shall it be seasoned? It is neither fit for the land, nor yet for the dunghill; but men cast it out. He that has ears to hear, let him hear.

Moral of the story: Count the costs and decide before the opportunity arises, not of what you will say, but whether you will accept the invitation to speak at all. For one cannot strive both for the honor of Men and of God.

Most of us would rather wait for bread to fall from the sky than to sell all that we have and give to the poor. But Jesus clearly required his followers not only to relinquish, but to detest, the inequities of this world. While fasting in the wilderness (just before beginning his ministry) Jesus feverishly relinquished the desires of the flesh. Although raised in a Jewish household, Jesus relinquished religious dogma (status symbols, individualistic yearnings for status, etc.) along with anything else that stood between him and his vision for peace and compassion (Kingdom of heaven) on earth. In order to advance the joys of heavenly bliss, we too must first relinquish our earthly toys.

The more one contemplates the unjust nature of this realm as Jesus did in the wilderness, the more they too will feverishly long to separate from it. In striving to thrive in a system of "haves" and have "nots," one expressly concedes to its inequitable terms and conditions (possession works both ways). One is either striving for what is of God (Good) or what is of the devil (evil). There is no middle ground (See weblink at Rationalbible.com, "For Us or Against Us"). Never before has there been or ever will be again, a greater opportunity than present to serve the Kingdom. The media world is virtually flattened with social platforms and networking opportunities like Facebook, YouTube, Google Plus, Twitter, Yahoo Answers, etc. The average citizen has access to the world with only the push of a button.

Again, the web is not limited to self-embellishment. Anyone who desires a social media platform can have it. Why then, do so few light-bearers utilize it? Quite simply, we hesitate for fear of losing our foothold on the very ladder we wish to tear down. There can be no disparity (social or economic inequality) in heaven. But why are we so fixed on impressing people that are just as spiritually dead and purposeless as we are? Jesus often told his disciple to give the cynics no mind. Their ceaseless jeers can only further the cause. Anyone who cannot see the value of saving lives can take a flying leap.

"Let them alone: they be blind leaders of the blind. And if the blind lead the blind, both shall fall into the ditch."
–Matthew 15:14

Ephraim is joined to idols: let him alone.

Hosea 4:17

"He is proud, knowing nothing, but doting about questions and strifes of words, whereof cometh envy, strife, railings, evil surmisings, perverse disputings of men of corrupt minds, and destitute of the truth, supposing that gain is godliness: from such withdraw thyself. But godliness with contentment is great gain. For we brought nothing into this world, and it is certain we can carry nothing out. And having food and raiment let us be therewith content. But they that will be rich fall into temptation and a snare, and into many foolish and hurtful lusts, which drown men in destruction and perdition. For the love of money is the root of all evil, which while some coveted after, they have erred from the faith, and pierced themselves through with many sorrows. But thou, O man of God, *flee these things; and follow after righteousness,* godliness, faith, love, patience, meekness. Fight the good fight of faith, lay hold on eternal life, whereunto thou art also called, and hast professed a good profession *before many witnesses."*

-1Timothy 6:4-12

It's been said that if slaughter houses had glass walls, the whole world would be vegetarian. Well, they don't! While the killing goes on behind closed doors there's hardly a mile of highway that doesn't advertise a thick "juicy" slab of meat for less than a gallon of gas. I've heard it said that the children of the coming Age would not tolerate the torture rooted in their "happy" meals if only afforded the truth. But the government will continue subsidizing this barbaric and otherwise profitless industry until enough people take a stand against it. Our Forests will continue to be cut down and overgrazed for the sake of the fast-food dollar menu so long as care what the self-righteous flesh feeder might think of us. After all, it's much more compelling to just fit in and call ourselves "Christian" as other hypocrites do.

Few people would refuse ringing a bell for the Salvation Army or donate toys for the needy children on Christmas. In this way, we not only get to appease a year's worth of guilt, we get social satisfaction from the admiring gazes of people who will never truly know us. How could they? We hide behind our masks, never revealing our innermost values or speaking up for what we truly believe. Who cares to be a voice for the voiceless when running the community "toy drive" is so much more fun (and socially acceptable) anyways?

We prefer the orthodox account that Jesus fed 5000 people with magic because it lets us mortals off the hook. We know children are dying from hunger and that grain grown on their land is wastefully diverted to "animal crops," etc. But we have our own problems to worry about, right? We live as though all we can do is pray for a miracle and have faith that God's "will be done as it is in heaven." Miracles are good, but inconsistent by nature. Jesus and his disciples worked tirelessly advancing the Kingdom. And when they needed to regroup, they sought seclusion. Even then, they ministered to those who came and gave all that they had. Imagine how miniscule the portions of bread (small as a seed) must have been. But it was more than enough to sow the spark of compassion. Those fortunate enough to have brought food into the wilderness gave to their hungry brothers and sisters. No greater miracle is needed.

The religionists could not understand the value of "Kingdom" Jesus envisioned. Rather, they said he was possessed of the devil. But he did not concerned himself with the high-minded people no matter their social standing. Jesus called on the "poor of spirit," not the social elite to help advance the Kingdom.

"Blessed are the poor in spirit: for theirs is the kingdom of heaven."

— Matthew 5:3

"The Spirit of the Lord GOD is upon me; because the LORD hath anointed me to preach good tidings unto the meek; he hath sent me to bind up the brokenhearted, to proclaim liberty to the captives, and the opening of the prison to them that are bound"

—Luke 4:18 (Isaiah 61:1)

"At that time Jesus answered and said, I thank thee, O Father, Lord of heaven and earth, because thou hast hid these things from the wise and prudent, and hast revealed them unto babes."

— Matthew 11:25

"At the same time came the disciples unto Jesus, saying, Who is the greatest in the kingdom of heaven? And Jesus called a little child unto him, and set him in the midst of them, And said, Verily I say unto you, Except ye be converted, and become as little children, ye shall not enter into the kingdom of heaven. Whosoever therefore shall humble himself as this little child, the same is greatest in the kingdom of heaven."

– Matthew 18:1–4

Because Jesus relinquished the glory of men in favor of the Kingdom, he was not swayed by the religionist's opinion of him. On the contrary, Jesus seems to have had a knack for saying things that seemed to contradict what was expected of a "righteous" man. In the book of Luke [16:1-31] we are told that Jesus told the following parable to his disciples within earshot of some wealthy but self-righteous dignitaries:

Jesus: There was a certain rich man, whose steward had been accused of wasting his fortune. So he called for him and said, "How is it that I hear this of thee? Turn in to me the records of your accounts; for you will no longer be a steward.

Jesus Continues: Then the steward thought to himself, "What shall I do, for my Lord has taken my stewardship from me? I cannot dig and I'm too proud to beg. I have decided what I must do so that, when I am completely put out of the stewardship, they may receive me into their houses." So he called each of his Lord's debtors to him and said unto the first, "How much do you owe my Lord?" The first debtor said, "One hundred barrels of oil." The steward said, "Take your bill. Sit down quickly and change it to 50." Then the steward called another debtor saying, "And how much do you owe? The second debtor said, "A hundred measures of wheat." The steward then said to the second debtor, "Take your bill, and write 40.

When the Master learned of what the unjust steward had done, he commended him for acting wisely; for the children of this world are in their generation wiser than the children of light.

Note: At this point, I'm sure the wealthy do-gooders were saying amongst themselves, "whaaaaaaaaaat!" They wanted so badly to feel justified in their plot to kill Jesus. And he gave them what they sought.

Jesus continues: Be faithful with the mammon of unrighteousness so that when it is gone, you will not be found wanting. He that is faithful with that which is least is faithful also in much. If therefore you have not faithfully used unrighteous mammon, who will commit to your trust the true riches? In other words, if you have not been faithful in that which is another man's, who shall give you that which is your own? No servant can serve two masters; for either he will hate the one, and love the other; or else he will hold to the one, and despise the other. You cannot serve both God and mammon.

At this point, the covetous religionists, who had heard could no longer hold their peace. They derided Jesus openly...

Jesus: You are among those which justify themselves before men but God knows your hearts; for that which is highly esteemed among men is an abomination in the sight of God.

Jesus version of good stewardship was literally a world apart from anything the wealthy religionist had ever encountered. It was more akin to a briefing on how to properly dispose of toxic refuse than a spiritual teaching! The wealthy religionists were left dumbfounded by this eccentric rabbi who (in their minds) openly praised a thief!

Truthfully, my own initial impulse was to disregard the parable of the "good steward" as a just another forgery. Jesus professed to a life of austerity. He told his followers to give all that they had to those in need, but not for the purpose of receiving favor! The next day it hit me. I felt like one of those cartoon characters again (whose eyes or temples pop out of my head accompanied by the sound of a whistle). I quickly wrote,

"I am not my thoughts. I am the observer"

I may be under the influences of my earthly flesh (my mortal master) but **I** am in control of its resources. I have the power to determine what is eternally good and to relinquish to my advantage. With this realization, the following verses took on new meaning:

Jesus: Your eyes are like a window for your body. When they are good, you have all the light you need. But when your eyes are bad, everything is dark. If the light inside you is dark, you surely are in the dark.

–Matthew 6:22–23

Jesus touched their eyes and said, "Because of your faith, you will be healed."

–Matthew 9:29

"All of them have stubborn minds! Their ears are stopped up, and their eyes are covered. They cannot see or hear or understand. If they could, they would turn to me, and I would heal them."

–Matthew 13:15

"But God has blessed you, because your eyes can see and your ears can hear!"

–Matthew 13:16

"If your eye causes you to sin, poke it out and get rid of it. You would be better off to go into life with only one eye than to have two eyes and be thrown into the funeral pyre of Hinnom. "

-Matthew 18:9

"They say unto him, Lord, that our eyes may be opened. Jesus felt sorry for them and touched their eyes. Right away they could see, and they became his followers."

-Matthew 20:33-34

"If your eye causes you to sin, get rid of it. You would be better off to go into God's kingdom with only one eye than to have two eyes and be thrown into hell."

-Mark 9:47

"Jesus told him, "You may go. Your eyes are healed because of your faith." Right away the man could see, and he went down the road with Jesus."

-Mark 10:52

"Are your eyes blind and your ears deaf? Don't you remember? How many baskets of leftovers you picked up when I fed those five thousand people with only five small loaves of bread?" "Yes," the disciples answered. "There were twelve baskets." Jesus then asked, "And how many baskets of leftovers did you pick up when I broke seven small loaves of bread for those four thousand people?" "Seven," they answered. "Don't you know what I am talking about by now?" Jesus asked. As Jesus and his disciples were going into Bethsaida, some people brought a blind man to him and begged him to touch the man. Jesus took him by the hand and led him out of the village, where he spit into the man's eyes. He placed his hands on the blind man and asked him if he could see anything. The man looked up and said, "I see people, but they look like trees walking around." Once again Jesus placed his hands on the man's eyes, and this time the man stared. His eyes were healed, and he saw everything clearly."

–Mark 8:18-25

"And he turned him unto his disciples, and said privately, Blessed are the eyes which see the things that ye see:"

–Luke 10:23

"Your eyes are the lamp for your body. When your eyes are good, you have all the light you need. But when your eyes are bad, everything is dark."

–Luke 11:34

"Jesus replied, "Look and you will see! Your eyes are healed because of your faith."

-Luke 18:42

"Say not ye, There are yet four months, and then cometh harvest? behold, I say unto you, Lift up your eyes, and look on the fields; for they are white already to harvest."

-John 4:35

"They asked the man, "What do you say about this one who healed your eyes?" "He is a prophet!" the man told them."

-John 9:17

I've found that my weaknesses stem from identifying with the thoughts and desires of my flesh rather than the Spirit. Again I'm reminded of the unjust steward whose mentor is quitting him. A wise Man acts with a sense of urgency once forewarned that his old life has been condemned...

When it is evening, ye say, It will be fair weather: for the sky is red. And in the morning, It will be foul weather today: for the sky is red and lowering. O ye hypocrites, ye can discern the face of the sky; but can ye not discern the signs of the times?"

-Matthew 16:1-4

The unjust steward in the parable is not distracted by what "has" or "should have" been. He has assessed the situation properly and reacted with a sense of urgency to preserve what mattered most to him. In the real world, an employer is more likely to conceal any intentions to fire unjust staff, for fear of how much more destructive a disgruntled employee might be. For this same purpose, the "eyes" of my body hide its many flaws and signs of decay that I might further identify with it. But because my heart belongs to those suffering souls in their loathsome cages and of my children left to suffer the environment in the aftermath of our destruction, my eyes will no longer be deceived.

> "And ye shall know the truth, and the truth shall make you free."
>
> –John 8.32.

Unlike the pompous publicans whose livelihood depended on them looking good in the eyes of the public, Jesus seized every opportunity to teach despite potential harms to his reputation. The religionists, blinded by their wealth and status mocked Jesus when he had said, "The master praised his unjust steward for looking out for himself so well. That's how it is! The people of this world look out for themselves better than the people who belong to the light." They missed the message because they only wanted to condemn the messenger.

Jesus didn't try to justify himself in their eyes. Rather, the essence of his message to them was clear, "Man may be concerned only with how you look on the outside, but God sees what is in your heart. The things that most people think are important are worthless as far as God is concerned."

Many times, he seems to have gone out of his way to shock and engage the judgmental listener. He didn't gild his parables with politically correct verbiage; quite the contrary. Nothing Jesus did could be construed as an appeal to popular opinion. As secular Christians, we shouldn't think that just because something is "normal" or acceptable, that it is just either. When Jesus walked into the temple in Jerusalem, freed the sacrificial animals and flipped the merchants tables... that certainly wasn't normal or acceptable.

It was akin to going to the world's largest church sanctioned potluck dinner and flipping the meat dishes while quoting scripture. (see, Appendix D: Scriptures on the Eating of Flesh) Or maybe the dismay of a Christian family who called on a recently converted vegan to "bless" their fowl Thanksgiving carcass. Only this unabashed activist didn't pray as others do, with fancy trimmings and empty words. Rather, she fully acknowledged the life that was violently taken for the family's pleasure and enjoyment!

"And while the flesh was yet between their teeth, ere it was chewed, the wrath of the LORD was kindled against the people, and the LORD smote the people with a very great plague."

–Numbers 11.33

We've all failed the call of the spirit at one time or another. In situations like the one's described above, we most often just observe the carnage and privately pray for forgiveness. Our failure to act is not always seen as a lack of courage but guised as respect for our elders and siblings. That is why Jesus told his followers to weigh the cost in advance. Not that acting out is always the answer. When you visit with family and friends, respectfully let them know where you stand on animal rights. Nothing's worse for animal rights than an activist who acts or speaks with righteous indignation.

Respectfully decline invitations to church and family functions where flesh is consumed. But let your stance be lovingly known. More important than your words and your actions are the motives behind them. In all your endeavors, keep your mind centered on the ultimate goal of animal liberation rather than the urge to exalt your esteem. Your intentions are the fulcrum from which all decisions are weighed. This is why Jesus stressed the importance of humbling oneself. What is perceived by Man to be weakness is indeed, her greatest strengths.

Now the man Moses was very meek, above all the men which were upon the face of the earth.

-Numbers 12.3

Blessed are the meek: for they shall inherit the earth.

- Matthew 5.5

Take my yoke upon you, and learn of me; for I am meek and lowly in heart: and ye shall find rest unto your souls. For my yoke is easy, and my burden is light.

-Matthew 11.29-30

Tell ye the daughter of Sion, Behold, thy King cometh unto thee, meek, and sitting upon an ass, and a colt the foal of an ass.

-Matthew 21.5

"The meek shall eat and be satisfied: they shall praise the LORD that seek him: your heart shall live forever."

-Psalms 22.26

"The humble shall see this, and be glad: and your heart shall live that seek God."

-Psalms 34.2

"My soul shall make her boast in the LORD: the humble shall hear thereof, and be glad."

-Psalms 69.32

"I acknowledged my sin unto thee, and mine iniquity have I not hid. I said, I will confess my transgressions unto the LORD; and thou forgavest the iniquity of my sin. Selah."

–Psalms 32:5

"For I will declare mine iniquity; I will be sorry for my sin."

–Psalms 38:18

"Wash me throughly from mine iniquity, and cleanse me from my sin."

–Psalms 51:2

"For I acknowledge my transgressions: and my sin is ever before me."

–Psalms 51:3

Don't be concerned about what others may think of you. Opinions are fickle, especially the public variety. Jesus relinquished status, as should we all. Remember what Jesus said to the religionists who gawked at him asking his disciples why they ate with tax collectors and sinners? He didn't resist their evil insinuations by trying to justify his himself. Rather, he seized the opportunity to deliver a message, "They that be whole need not a physician, but they that are sick. But go ye and learn what that meaneth, I will have mercy, and not sacrifice: for I am not come to call the righteous, but sinners to repentance."

When it comes to our finances, we know exactly what is expected of us and we act accordingly. As for our moral and ethical duties however, we act without purpose or urgency. We are simply too busy, as the saying goes, "keeping up with the Joneses" to consider the plight of our suffering and defenseless animal cousins (yes, I went there). All major spiritual traditions at inception, recognized that all creature have an equal right to life.

"…All meats eaten by living beings are of their own relatives"

_ Lankavatara Sutra (Tripitaka No. 671)

At what stage of moral development will the human race acknowledge that the other animals aren't put here just for them to eat? Perhaps, we are put here to evolve a better understanding of mercy and compassion from living together. When I was a child, my family slaughtered animals for the purpose of harvesting the meat from their bones. During the summer months, we had a garden and produce markets were even more commonplace than they are today. Though these more healthful, less gruesome options were plentiful, we never once thought a meal complete without meat. We certainly never considered the animal's right to life.

We didn't think about whether it was morally wrong to murder an animal just for the sake of our perverse palates. Our preacher craved fried chicken almost as much as the Pharisees loved their wealth and status. Of course, our religion didn't forbid it so long as we gave our "blessings" before eating. Not a full eulogy of course. It would have been impossible to discern from which individual body came the chunk of flesh at the end of either fork.

"In matters of conscience, the law of the majority has no place… The greatness of a nation and its moral progress can be judged by the way its animals are treated."

–Gandhi

Getting back to the virtue of humility; it seems to be the key to advancing the Kingdom. When it came to a life heroic activism, Jesus seemed virtually fearless. But when it came to verbal praise, he avoided it like the plague. The books of Matthew[19:16-30], Mark [10:14-24], and Luke [18:18-30] record that Jesus was once approached by someone addressed him as, "Good Master." The first thing Jesus did was deflect the compliment...

Jesus: Why do you call me good? There is none good but one, and that is God...

Jesus adamantly refused the "glory of Men" choosing rather, to glorify first that which is good in Man.

If God be glorified in him, God shall also glorify him in himself, and shall straightway glorify him.

–John 13:32

As for the young religionist's assertion of a life thereafter...

"If you wish to enter into life, keep the commandments"

One who wishes to extend an inequitable existence however, toils in vain.

Jesus: He who sins is the slave of sin.

To serve a purpose worth dying for is to be free from the perverse constraints of the flesh ...

Jesus; For whosoever will save his life shall lose it; but whosoever will lose his life for the sake of the Kingdom, the same shall save it."

Jesus told the man that the way to enter into life is to keep the commandments...

"Thou shalt not commit murder.

Thou shalt not commit adultery.

Thou shalt not steal.

Thou shalt not bear false witness.

Honour thy father and your mother; and,

Thou shalt love thy neighbor as thyself."

To the young man's credit, he approached Jesus with respect using the title "didaskale agathe" (διδάσκαλος) which means doctor or teacher. It is similar to the way Nicodemus greeted him, "You are a Teacher sent from God." The fact that the man was both young and wealthy implies that he was wise beyond his years. It never fails to elicit an emotional response for me, to consider the stark contrast between Jesus' modest dress to that of the young man's fine linens. The young man's retort indicates that he has kept the commandments from childhood on but still couldn't see the Kingdom. He asks Jesus, "What then, am I failing to do?"

Jesus probably looks at the young man's elegant upper-class attire, smiles and responds accordingly...

Jesus: If thou wilt be whole, go and sell all that you have and give to the poor and you shalt have treasure in heaven. Then come and follow me.

Obviously, the man came by his wealth in good conscience. By most standards, the young man had done everything right. But he had yet to see the Kingdom that Jesus so vividly described. When Jesus told him that he had to give even that up however, he sorrowful walked away. Jesus turned to his disciples and said:

"How hardly shall they that have riches enter into the kingdom of God!"

The disciples were astonished by what Jesus had said about this young man he so clearly loved, someone who kept the commandments without fail. But Jesus repeated the sentiment...

Jesus: Children, how hard is it for them that trust in riches to enter into the kingdom of God!

"It is easier for a camel to go through the eye of a needle, than for a rich man to enter into the kingdom of God."

At this point, the disciples were disappointed beyond words, saying to themselves, "Who then can be saved?" But Jesus heard them. Looking upon them he offered them the secret...

Jesus: With men it is impossible, but not with God; for with God all things are possible.

Peter: Look, we have left everything and followed you.

"There is no person who has left their house, or brethren, or sisters, or father, or mother, or wife, or children, or lands, for the sake of the Kingdom who has not received a hundredfold NOW in THIS MOMENT."

Note: In Matthew's 19:30 rendering, Jesus is alleged to have told Peter that those who have followed him will be rewarded in the "regeneration" (en teî palingenesiaî) which means, "the new birth of the world." The term was a common term among the Stoics and the Pythagoreans as well as many mystery cults. (Angus, Mystery Religions and Christianity, pp. 95). The reference to Jesus' disciples sitting on twelve thrones as judges of Israel however, is yet another obvious forgery. Judging from Mark's 10:28-31 rendering, we find that Jesus probably chastised Peter for such a comment ...

Jesus: "But many that are first shall be last; and the last first."

Jesus follows up with a parable relating the Kingdom of Heaven "to a man who, in the early morning, went out to hire some workers for his vineyard..." He hired at the rate of one denarius, which was a generous day's pay equal to that of a Roman soldier. Now, the owner of the vineyard returns to the marketplace and hires laborers three more times over the course of the working day. Only, he agreed to pay them, "whatever is right." The iniquitous scene is sadly reminiscent of a modern day Home Depot parking lot. Of course, the veteran workers complained saying, "these who were hired last, worked only one hour, and you have made them equal to us who have borne the burden of the work and the heat of the day!'(See also, pg. 192 of the poor widow who gave all that she had.) The vineyard keeper replied saying ...

'I am not being unfair to you, friend. Didn't you agree to work for a denarius? Take your pay and go. I want to give the one who was hired last the same as I gave you. Don't I have the right to do what I want with my own money? Or are you envious because I am generous?'

Jesus: So the last will be first, and the first will be last."

We miss the Kingdom for wanting what is "rightfully" due. A mentor of mine once said condescendingly, "It's okay to build castles in the sky so long as you don't move into them!" Jesus kept said something to that effect also...

"He then said, "Watch out that you are not led astray, for many will come in my name saying, 'I am the one and, 'The time has drawn near.' So do not go after them. "

-Luke 21:8

We would naturally suspect a preacher who continuously lectures on tithing, but what of less apparent motivators (status, social recognition, etc.). Contemporary psychology confirms the long-held suspicion that extrinsic rewards (gold stars, promises of favor in the afterlife, etc.) diminish the intrinsic value (immediate joy) of an otherwise gratifying task. That is, we sacrifice the Kingdom (true life) to the extent that we strive for uncertain future rewards (streets of gold, glory of Man, etc.). Jesus said that heaven is not some faraway place in the hereafter. He wanted his disciples to obtain joy from purpose-filled servitude in the here and now.

Neither shall they say, Lo here! or, lo there! for, behold, the kingdom of God is within you.

-Luke 17:21

"For whosoever will save his life shall lose it: and whosoever will lose his life for my sake shall find it. "

-Matthew 16:25

"And he saith unto them, Is it lawful to do good on the sabbath days, or to do evil? to save life, or to kill? But they held their peace. "

-Mark 3:4

"For whosoever will save his life shall lose it; but whosoever shall lose his life for my sake and the gospel's, the same shall save it. "

-Mark 8:35

"Then said Jesus unto them, I will ask you one thing; Is it lawful on the sabbath days to do good, or to do evil? to save life, or to destroy it? "

-Luke 6:9

"For whosoever will save his life shall lose it: but whosoever will lose his life for my sake, the same shall save it. "

-Luke 9:24

"Whosoever shall seek to preserve his life shall lose it; and whosoever shall relinquish his life shall preserve it. "

-Luke 17:33

This is to say that whosoever would seek to preserve their illusory lives will inevitably lose it. But those who would gladly relinquish their inequitable existence for the sake of the Kingdom shall experience true life here and now.

The Gospels report that Jesus relied on the source (truth) to tell him what to say Luke 12:12; 21:15. Time and time again, we find the parables chillingly contradict the suspect text which precede them. It's as if the Spirit is saying...

"So do not be afraid of them. Because there isn't any covered over that won't be uncovered, and there's nothing hidden that won't be known."

The book of Mark 10:35-45 and Matthew 20:21-28 collectively record that James and John asked Jesus how they could secure his favor so that they might sit, "one on thy right hand, and the other on thy left hand, in thy glory." But Jesus sat them down in private...

Jesus: You know not what you ask when you say, "drink of the cup" that I drink of. You don't want the baptism that I am to be baptized with?

James or John: But we are willing.

Jesus: To sit on either on my right hand or on my left is not mine to give; but it shall be given to them for whom it is prepared.

When the other disciples heard of what James and John had done, they were very displeased. So Jesus called them all to him...

Jesus: You know that those who are deemed to rule over the Gentiles exercise lordship over them, and their high ranking people exercise authority above them. But it will not be like this among you, but whoever wishes to be great among you must be your servant, and whoever of you wishes to be first must be the servant of all.

The book of Luke ^{chapter 19:1-27} reports of a rich tax collector named Zacchaeus who had heard of the Kingdom teachings and believed it to be true. Learning that Jesus would be passing through his hometown of Jericho. Zacchaeus wished to see Jesus but, being a relatively short man, he feared he wouldn't be able to see above the crowd. So he ran ahead and climbed up into a sycamore tree. When Jesus got to where Zacchaeus was, he looked up and said:

"Hurry down! I want to stay with you today."

So Zacchaeus hurried down and welcomed Jesus gladly. Some people in the crowd grumbled...

"But this man Zacchaeus, he is a sinner!

"...And Jesus is going home to eat with him"

Later that day however, Zacchaeus made an announcement:

"I pledge half of my goods as a gift to the poor; and if I have taken anything from any man by false accusation,

I restore him fourfold."

Note: Jericho was a highly populated center of trade which explains the crowd in addition to Zacchaeus' wealth. As explained earlier, tax collectors like Zacchaeus were employed by the occupying Roman government but charged (at their discretion) their fee to the taxpayer directly. Failure to comply carried dire penalties. Needless to say, Zacchaeus would have been loathed by his fellow Jews. But when Jesus saw Zacchaeus, he didn't see what everyone else saw. Instead of a loathsome tax collector, Jesus saw a man who would not be denied based on his lowly stature.

Remember also than any person caught associating with publicans and sinners would be considered unclean and ostracized by the religious community. But Jesus didn't care for such things. His message was simple: love and mercy (true equality) above all else. The religionists perceived Jesus as a threat to their esteemed positions. They deemed his teachings, the work of the devil.

Jesus, I grieve for you, religionists! For you tithe the mint and rue and all manner of herbs, and push aside reason and the love of God.

Jesus stirred up the people and for the high priests and religious professors of the Law that was bad for business. This dynamic, on a psycho-social level is intimately familiar to each of us. It's not that we don't have desire the end of violence, we know with every fiber of our being that is our purpose for existence. Many people tell me that they simply have too many "irons in the fire" to protest injustice. But "being busy" is no excuse. Most of us have only one priority, to protect our feeble reputations. But a spotless reputation like any other tool has yet to serve a meaningful purpose. Remember Jesus' parable of the unjust steward? It's time we ask ourselves what the Hell we're saving our pristine public and self-images for. Those hypocrites that Jesus kept harping on... that's us!

Why do we pretend to be something we aren't? More dramatically stated: why do we trade our birthrights for the fickle acceptance of similarly despondent others, knowing full well that we do not truly live alongside pretense. One is truly alive, only when their actions reflect their true nature, good or bad. But to be both alive and free, one must become immune to the influences of the flesh. A stated goal of the non-hypocrite then, might be to remain untethered by the illusions of this realm.

The pressures of day to day life play a meaningful role in that they reveal one's true allegiances. Jesus maintained composure even amidst the advances of those who wished to kill him! He waited for the spirit to provide the words and only then did he speak. See Matthew 10:19-20, 10:27, 12:34, 13:11; Luke 11:53-54, 12:1-12; John 4:26, 6:63, 7:17, 8:26-28, 8:38, 12:49-50, 14:10, 16:13 Even during his trial, Jesus refused to speak until led by the spirit to do so. And when Jesus finally spoke, it was not to resist the evil charges brought against him. Matthew 27:12-14 He had weighted the cost far in advance...

Jesus: My friends, be not afraid of those that kill the body. After that, they can do no more harm. When they bring you into the synagogues, and in front of the magistrates and other powers, take no mind of it whatsoever. Don't think about what how you will answer or what you will say. The Holy Spirit will teach you in that moment what you need to say.

Jesus did not allow the cares of his earthly life to obstruct his vision for a compassionate world. He sought refuge not for fear of powerful religionist detractors, but for his immense love for them. Their lack of sincerity must have pained him greatly in that they were snared by their love of status.

Jesus: I grieve for you religionists! You so love the uppermost seats in the synagogues, and greetings in the markets.

"I grieve for you hypocritical scribes and Pharisees! For you are like graves which are not apparent to the men who walk over them are not aware."

"Woe unto you professors of the Law! For you laden with burdens too grievous to be borne and yet you do not touch them with even one of your fingers."

"I grieve for you! For you build the sepulchers for the prophets whom your fathers killed."

Jesus' portrayal of the ancient hypocrite bears a surprising resemblance to contemporary religionists who scramble his teachings with theological absurdities. Are we to believe that a man who so fervently <u>crusaded against, sacrificial offerings</u> was actually the embodiment of God who literally washed people's sins away with his blood?

"Woe unto you, professors of the Law! For you have taken away the key of knowledge. Not only did you not enter, you hindered those that would have done so."

On Wealth & Status

"Every valley shall be filled, and every mountain and hill shall be brought low; and the crooked shall be made straight, and the rough ways shall be made smooth."

–John the Baptist

Jesus taught that one cannot serve two masters. If a person strives to thrive in an unjust world, he or she will do so at the cost of the ideal (Kingdom of Heaven). Jesus seized every opportunity to teach the value of austerity, not for the sake of suffering but to clear a path for righteous thought and action. What person, valuing earthly wealth above all else, will give freely to those in need or protest an injustice? A man once said to Jesus, "Lord, I will follow you wherever you may go." But then Jesus reminded the hopeful activist of how he had no earthly ties ...

Jesus: Foxes have holes, and birds of the air have nests; but the Son of man has no place to lay his head.

Still another indicated a desire to follow. He told Jesus that he only needed to bury his dead or dying father first.

Jesus: Let the dead bury their dead. Go now and preach the Kingdom of God.

A third would-be activist said "Lord, I will follow thee; but let me first go and bid farewell to my family."

Jesus: No man, having put his hand to the plough, and looking back, is fit for the Kingdom of God.

We must remain unfettered by anything other than the furrow we are driving. Should we hesitate to consider the personal costs, we risk losing sight of those who matter most: the future inhabitants of our planet. (See weblink at Rationalbible.com, "The Real Price of Meat")

Focus on the Message

As Jesus addressed a crowd, someone mentioned the recent massacring of Galileans led by Judas Gaulonitis (Judas of Galilee, Acts 5:37) in the near vicinity. They were killed for refusing to give tribute to Ceasar, for it was prohibited by Mosaic Law. Pilate, the governor of Judea at the time, sent a throng of soldiers who massacred the group during the feast of the Passover as they offered their sacrifices in the temple.

Religionists: This is the anniversary of the Galileans whose blood Pilate mingled with their sacrifices.

The Bible hints that the religionists whom Jesus had just deemed hypocrites, tried to entrap him by this, either to condemn himself to Pilot or to his fellow Jews. But Jesus' was not concerned about articulating the perfect response Luke 12:11-12 He simply neutralized the ploy and used it as a platform to engage the reluctant activist listeners:

Jesus: Are you supposing that these Galileans were sinners above all others because they suffered such things? What about the eighteen, upon whom the tower in Siloam fell and slew them. Do you think that they were sinners above all those who lived in Jerusalem? I think not. If you do obey the Spirit, you will all likewise perish as if you had never lived.

Then Jesus told them the parable of the fig tree.

Jesus: A certain man had a fig tree planted in his vineyard. But when he sought fruit from it, he found none. So the man said to the dresser of his vineyard, "Behold, for the last three years I came seeking fruit on this fig tree, and find none. It is better to cut it down than to cumbereth it the ground?" But the vineworker pleaded on behalf of the tree saying, "Lord, let it alone this year also, for I will till the soil about and fertilize it" If it does not bear fruit after this, then we can cut it down."

At this point, you've probably noticed that the New Testament cites the "fig tree" reference both as a parable and as real life events (See also: p. 126 & 252-258). It is equally likely however that these reoccurring themes began as single allegorical myths. Regardless of the historical accuracy of the NT teachings, the takeaway lesson is that we shouldn't squander what insights of truth we have. Like the man in Jesus' parable in Luke[12:16-20] who built larger and larger barns to store his wealth, we squander our true riches in striving for the illusory in that they bring us further from our purpose. We know not the minute nor the hour of our deaths. The real question for the Ages is "How many more lifetimes of wasted opportunity and destruction can the planet withstand?" See, Matthew16:3 & Luke12:56

"Live as if you were to die tomorrow. Learn as if you were to live forever."

"The greatness of humanity is not in being human, but in being humane." "In a gentle way, you can shake the world." "Change yourself – you are in control." "I will not let anyone walk through my mind with their dirty feet." *"The weak can never forgive. Forgiveness is the attribute of the strong."* "Freedom is not worth having if it does not include the freedom to make mistakes." "We need not wait to see what others do." "A 'No' uttered from the deepest conviction is better than a 'Yes' merely uttered to please, or worse, to avoid trouble." *"To call woman the weaker sex is a libel: it is man's injustice to woman."* "Earth provides enough to sa... ve as if you were to die tomorrow. Learn as if you were to live forever."

The greatness of humanity is not in being human, but in being humane." "In a gentle way, you can shake the world." "Change yourself – you are in control." "I will not let anyone walk through my mind with their dirty feet." *"The weak can never forgive. Forgiveness is the attribute of the strong."* "Freedom is not worth having if it does not include the freedom to make mistakes." "We need not wait to see what others do." "A 'No' uttered from the deepest conviction is better than a 'Yes' merely uttered to please, or worse, to avoid trouble." *"To call woman the weaker sex is a libel: it is man's injustice to woman."* "Earth provides enough to satisfy every man's needs, but not every man's greed." "Live as if you were to die tomorrow. Learn as if you were to live forever." **"The greatness of humanity is not in being human, but in being humane."** "In a gentle way, you can shake the world." "Change yourself – you are in control." "I will not let anyone walk through my mind with their dirty

The Last Days

It was time for the traditional Feast of Tabernacles (Festival of Shelters). The chief priests and religionist professors of the Law in Judea got together to plan how they might have Jesus arrested and put to death. But Jesus was led by the Spirit to bid his family farewell in Galilee. Jesus' brothers attempted to goad him into attending despite his apprehensions...

Jesus' brothers: You say that our methods of serving God are wrong and that you know how to better serve God. But no man does anything in secret that he wishes to be made known. Accompany us to the Feast in Judea, so that the people may see your works. You can declare before the world, that the teaching of Moses is wrong.

Jesus: My hour has yet to come; but you may at associate whenever and whomever you wish. The world does not hate you as they do me, because I stand in testimony against it, that its works are evil. For that reason, I will not go with you to the feast but I will not do so until led by the Spirit.

It is possible that Jesus misconstrued the fears and temptations of the flesh as the voice of the Spirit. Or maybe he felt led to go in secret. Perhaps he was like the older brother in Jesus' parable who said to his father, "I will not go" but later changed his mind and went...

Jesus, a man who had two sons. The father went to the older son and said, "Go work in the vineyard today!" His son told him that he would not go, but later changed his mind and went. The man then told his younger son to go work in the vineyard also. The boy said he would, but he never did. Which one of the sons obeyed the will of his father? "

The book of John records that the many who were present at the feast sought him out saying, "Where is he?" They began to argue in secret about whether he might truly be sent from God. Jesus finally made an appearance in the temple about midway through the celebration. He was teaching such that even the chief priests wondered amongst themselves, "How can this unlearned and unassuming man teach with such depth of understanding?"

Jesus: If any person will do the will of God, he shall know whether the Gospel I teach is of Man or revealed to him by the Spirit. He that speaks of his own teachings does so to exalt himself. But the one who seeks only to glorify the Kingdom speaks for righteousness sake. Besides, didn't Moses give the law to you, and yet none of you have kept it? Why then do you go about killing me?

Of course, those present were not yet privy to the ominous intentions of the chief priests. Someone yelled, "You're crazy! What makes you think someone wants to kill you?" Seemingly unfazed, Jesus kept addressing his adversaries openly...

Jesus: I have shown you but one work and ye all marvel. You accept that a boy should receive circumcision on the Sabbath day so that the customs of our fathers (not even Mosaic Law) should not be broken. Why then are you angry at me for having ministered to a man on the Sabbath day? Judge not according to popular opinion, but to eternal righteousness.

Note: In referencing the "one miracle" that Jesus performed in Jerusalem, the authors of this passage in John 7:21 -24 are referencing the healing of the infirm (superstitious) man at the pool of Bethesda on the Sabbath about a year and a half prior to this occasion. The "one miracle" which Jesus more often refers to in the canonical gospels however (best illustrates the true significance of the Kingdom) is the feeding of 5000 in a deserted area near Bethsaida Galilee. The simple fact that so many hungry people in a deserted place would unreservedly share what little food they have with complete strangers seems amazing especially by today's individualistic standards! Such a "miracle" attests today, more than ever, to the prudence of Jesus' Kingdom teachings.

Delivering the Message

Jesus' presence at the Feast of tabernacles had left a lasting impression on the people. One so alarming that the religionist officials resolved once and for all, to kill him. They issued orders that if anyone knew of his whereabouts, they must report it or face dire consequences. Yet Jesus was led again into the wilderness. This time, he went to a region near the city of Ephraim where he stayed with his disciples. With Passover less than a week away, many of the Jews had begun making encampments in Jerusalem. The people awaited Jesus' arrival in suspense whispering amongst themselves as to whether he would attend the feast this year.

As Jesus prepared for the trip to Jerusalem on Sunday morning, his disciples pleaded again that he might avert capture...

Jesus: Because I would relinquish my life, I receive it. No one can take from me, what is given willingly. This is my right as revealed to me by the Spirit. Be mindful of what spirit you are of also. Anyone can walk in the day without stumbling, because he sees the light of this world. But many stumble in the night because the light of the Kingdom does not shine forth from within them. If the children of God do not let their light shine, there will be only darkness.

First Palm Sunday

Jesus rode triumphantly into Jerusalem upon an ass with a colt in tow. People gathered all around to hear him speak. Even young children sat earnestly listening as Jesus ministered the Gospel of the Kingdom unto them. Many had lived their whole lives, never having considered such doctrines as purposeful humility and nonresistance though buried deep within the rubble of their beloved Judaic texts. Those who longed for the Kingdom were grateful for Jesus' teachings. But there where many also, that harbored the spirit of vengeance within their hearts. They were among those who unsuspectingly sided with the church officials who had secretly resolved to kill him. Jesus spent the night in Bethany.

Monday of Holy Week

On the way into Jerusalem, Jesus was hungry. He spots a fig tree growing leaves from afar off and eagerly approached hoping to find ripe fruit. Realizing that figs were not yet in season however, he seizes the opportunity to teach.

Jesus: We can learn a lesson from the fig tree. As soon as its branch become tender and it puts forth leaves, you know that summer is near. In this way, you can see from the happenings around you that the Kingdom of God is at hand. For as were the days of Noah, so will be the coming of the Kingdom. In those days right up to the flood people were eating drinking, marrying and giving in marriage. Until the day when Noah entered the ark and the flood came and swept them all away, they were unaware of what was afoot. So I it will be when the Kingdom of Heaven comes. Two men will be in the field; one will be taken and one left. Two women will be grinding at the mill; one will be taken and one left. Therefore, stay awake, for you do not know on what day your time is coming. But know this, if the master of the house had known what part of the night the thief was coming, he would have stayed awake and would not have let his house be broken into. You must also be ready, for the Son of Man is coming at an hour you do not expect.

Surely Jesus felt the prying eyes of the commercial religionists upon him as he entered Jerusalem, knowing full well that the even the slightest indiscretion would cost his mortal life. Yet he went into the temple and began flipping the tables of moneychangers as he'd done almost three years prior. While setting the animals free, he quoted Jeremiah[7:11] "...Is this house, which is called by my name, become a den of robbers in your eyes?" Of all the Christian commercial holiday traditions, none is conceivably more worthy than this.

When the chief officials came for Jesus, he seized the opportunity to chastise them publicly for capitalizing on the people's desire to serve God. He declared as heresy, the practice of animal sacrifice as an offering and defended his arguments with the Old Law in such a way that that they could not arrest him in the presence of the people.

While at the feast, Jesus' disciples feared that by talking with sinners and outcasts, he might turn the tide of public opinion against him. They knew that the religionist officials wanted to depict Jesus' teachings as a complete rejection of Mosaic Law, rather than a revival of it. And if that were to happen in a venue like this, Jesus would most assuredly lose the protections of the public. But he would let nothing impede his mission, which was to usher in the Kingdom of Heaven on earth.

Jesus knew all too well, the costs of his ministry. He had already relinquished the concerns of his illusory life while under the auspices of his cousin and mentor, John the Baptist. A man recently beheaded by the very people who now sought to take his own life. The Bible tells us that Jesus prayed that the cup might pass from his lips but that God's will be done. Tolstoy imagines it to have gone something like this:

"As a grain of wheat perishes to bring forth fruit, may I be willing for the sake of the Kingdom. Let the will of God be manifest through me now."

In that fateful moment, Jesus turned to the crowd and spoke openly of what he'd shared only with Nicodemus in private.

Jesus: We are the children of the Kingdom of heaven and our neighbors abroad are of one nation under God. But with our quarreling governments and religious creeds, we have lost our way. There is no need to conquer our brethren and divide ourselves from them.

The religionists: Are you suggesting that we abandon our covenant with God? Our prophets foretold of the coming of Christ on earth, but you speak only of a Kingdom from within the son of man. How are we to liken that to our teachings?

Jesus: In order to worship what is good, I tell you to seek the guidance of the Spirit. By this, I teach no new creed but present what all Men already know to be self-evident, that Man should reverence all life equally.

Many of the common folk believed what Jesus had said. But the majority of the affluent could not accept his teachings of social and economic equality because they cherished their wealth and status. They too became increasingly alarmed by the affect that Jesus was having on the people.

Tuesday of Holy Week

On the way back to Jerusalem, the disciples catch a glimpse of the now fabled fig tree from afar and jested amongst themselves of how the leaves had completely withered. Once they arrived, Jesus lectures extensively on the temple steps. Once again, he *abbreviates the 10 commandments into five*, beginning with the first: "Love your neighbor as thyself." Jesus asserts that his teaching reaffirm what is good of Old Law and must remain in effect until the Kingdom of God is reestablished on earth.

Jesus: In the old law, it written, "Do not kill…" and if one Man kills another, then his transgressor must be put to death also. But I teach that if one man grows angry with another, he is just as at fault. So, if we wish to pray, we should first consider our trespasses. Have you spoken abusively to your brother or your sister? If you can think of even one person who feels offended by you, get off your knees and go first to make peace with them. After that, you may pray.

We often get so caught up on being "right," even in our spiritual dealings, that we forget that God is Love and Truth. How can we expect to commune or pray to the very spirt we shun in favor of animosity? Jesus said that we should make peace before anything else.

Jesus asked, "If we love only those that love us back, what is our reward?" Everyone we encounter is someone's son or daughter and we should treat them with the same love and understanding we would afford a child of our own. Suppose an individual had never been loved and therefore cannot express it. Isn't that all the more reason to to do so? It is by comparison that we subjectify one another. (I may be bad, but they are worse... beautiful-ugly, skinny-fat, rich-poor, etc.). But true love is unconditional. This assertion relates to the second of Jesus' his five commandments: "Do not lust." As if by chance, some religionist hecklers interrupted Jesus' sermon asking if it was permitted for a man to divorce his wife.

Jesus: Have you not read that from the beginning, created God Man made both male and female? On account of this, a man will leave his father and his mother and will be joined to his wife, and the two will become united? They are no longer two, but have become one flesh. Therefore what God has joined together, no Man must put asunder."

Religionists: Why then did Moses command us to give a certificate of divorce and to divorce her?"

Jesus: Moses, with reference to Man's hardness of heart, permitted him to divorce his wife. But it was not this way from the beginning. Except for the basis of sexual immorality, a man should not divorce his wife.

Jesus' Disciples: If this be the lot of a man and his wife, it would be better not to marry at all!"

Jesus: Not everyone can maintain such single-minded vision. But to those whom it has been given – For there are eunuchs who were born as such from their mother's womb and there are eunuchs who were made eunuchs by people, and there are eunuchs who have made themselves such for the sake of the Kingdom of Heaven. The one who is able to receive such an understanding – let him accept it.

And then Jesus affirmed the third of his five commandments: "Do not take oaths." As if by chance again, some tax collectors came up to Peter asking, "Does your teacher not pay the double drachma tax?" Peter answered "Yes." But when he came into the house, Peter spoke with Jesus concerning the matter...

Jesus: What do you think, Simon? From whom do the kings of the earth collect tolls or taxes, from their own sons, or from foreigners?"

Peter: From foreigners

Jesus: Then we are the children not of this Kingdom. But so that we do not toil in the net of this world, give to them that ask.

Note: Many peace activists, as a form of civil disobedience, participate in what is known as "war tax resistance." Mahatma Gandhi led the great "Salt March" which is the most infamous tax resistance campaign in history. Other examples include the Women's Tax Resistance League in order to promote women's suffrage. Each proved effective.

Later in the day, the religionist officials sent spies pretending to be Jesus' followers that they might snare Jesus by his words. Either, he would condemn Caesar or himself to the civil authorities...

Religionists: "Teacher, we know that you are just and that you are impartial to persons. By your teachings, is it permitted for us to pay taxes to Caesar or not?"

Jesus, having no wealth of his own, asked to see a denarius.

Jesus: Whose image and inscription does it have?

Religionists: Caesar's

Jesus: Well then, give to Caesar what belongs to Caesar, and give to God that which is of God!"

Though the religionists failed to denounce Jesus publicly, they succeeded in dispelling the widespread belief that he was the Jewish people's long awaited warrior messiah who was to free them from the bondage of Rome.

At no time, did Jesus seek fame or fortune. His doctrine clearly called for the relinquishment of all personal possessions withholding only one's allegiance, which belongs firstly to the Kingdom of

God. The wolves (commercial religionists and publicans alike), divert what is of God, entrapping young minds for their own devices. Under the pressure social shaming, our children are forced to take befuddling oaths not only in the churches but in schoolyards. This is the very thing our forefathers wished to avoid when they insisted on the separation of church and state. Even so, public school children are conditioned to vow allegiance to the flag. Elementary school children pledge in advance (hand over heart) not only to lay down their lives for their government, but to take the lives of others in defense of it. What other purpose could such cradle to grave conditioning serve but to indoctrinate the lower castes to an unjust system? War is a luxury of the rich. Let each person be governed by their conscience. For in truth, there is but one nation under God: the Kingdom of Heaven.

No Man is free from the ravages of sin. It is for this reason that Jesus warned his followers, "judge not that they might not be judged." No one has been anointed by God to preside over another. As imperfect beings, we offend and take offense, despite even the best of intentions. With imperfect minds, we are simply not equipped to exact punishment according to harms. And this brings us to Jesus' reiteration of the fourth of his five commandments: "Do not resist and evil" person.

As if by chance yet again, some of Jesus' more determined religionist detractors drag before him, a woman who had allegedly been caught in the act of adultery.

Religionists: Teacher, this woman was caught in the very act of committing adultery! Now in the law, Moses commanded us to stone such women. So what do you say?"

Jesus, bent down and began to write with his finger on the ground as if having never heard the question. One assumes that Jesus paused to take counsel of the spirit. When they persisted in asking him, Jesus stood and said to them:

"The one of you without sin, let him throw the first stone at her!"

Then Jesus bent down and continued writing on the ground. The religionists, when they heard what Jesus had said, became convicted by their conscience. One by one, they began to depart, beginning with the elders until Jesus was left alone with the woman.

Jesus stood up again and spoke with the woman in private...

Jesus: What happened to your accusers? Does no one condemn you?

Adulteress: No one, Lord.

Jesus: Neither do I condemn you. Go, and be free from your sins.

This brings us to the final of Jesus' five commandments: "Love unconditionally." Jesus said that it wasn't enough to love those that love you back. He said that we should do well even to those whom would persecute us. As if by chance (yet again) a certain professor of Mosaic Law stood up to challenge Jesus saying, "Master, what shall I do to inherit eternal life?"

Jesus: What is your understanding of what is written in the law?

Mosaic Lawyer: Thou shalt love the Lord thy God with all thy heart, and with all thy soul, and with all thy strength, and with all thy mind Deuteronomy 6:5; 11:1,13,22; 13:3; 19:9; 30:6,16,20; Joshua 22:5; 23:11; Psalms 31:23; 97:10; 116:1; Matthew 22:37; Mark 12:30; Luke 10:27 and thy neighbor as thyself. Leviticus 19:18; Matthew 5:43; 19:19; 22:39; Mark 12:31;

Jesus: You have spoken well. Do this and you will know what it means to receive life.

The religionist professor hoping to further glorify himself in the eyes of those present said, "And who is my neighbor?" To which Jesus replied with the parable of the Good Samaritan.

Jesus: A Jewish man went down from Jerusalem to Jericho and fell among thieves. They stripped him of his clothes, wounded him and left him for dead. As if by chance, one of his countrymen came along and when he saw him, passed by on the other side. A neighboring Levite journeyed along, looked at the man and passed by on the other side as well. But then a Samaritan, a rival to the Jew happened along. And when he saw the man lying there by the road, he was overtaken with compassion. He went to the man and dressed his wounds and poured oil and wine over them. Then he set the man on his own horse and carried him to an inn to care for him further. And the following day, he took out two denarii and gave them to the innkeeper saying "Take care of him, and I will pay whatever debt is incurred, upon my return.

Jesus then asked the Lawyer which of the three men became a true neighbor to the man who fell among the robbers?"

Mosaic Lawyer: The one who showed mercy to him.

Jesus: This is how you should be also.

Then Jesus was approached by a group of Sadducees, who did not believe in resurrection nor understand the significance and immediacy of Jesus' unique perspective on the Kingdom.

Sadducees: Teacher, Moses decreed that if someone's brother dies having a wife but childless, that the survivor should take the wife and father her children. Now what if there were seven brothers, and the first took a wife and died childless. Then the second and the third took her, all the way to the seventh; all having died without children. Finally the woman also died. Now in the resurrection, whose wife of the seven will the woman be?

Jesus: The children of this Age marry and are given in marriage. But those who ascend the concerns of this realm will neither marry nor be given in marriage. Because as children of the Kingdom, they will never feel incomplete. Even Moses (in the passage about the bush) revealed the nature of resurrection when he calls his Lord, "the God of Abraham and the God of Isaac and the God of Jacob. Now he is not a God of the dead but of the living, for all live unto (αὖ by, in, into, of, adjoined with) Him!"

Jesus' statement illustrates an ancient belief that all life springs from an eternal source for which it will return. He referenced a passage in Shemoth Rabba which can be found in Exodus 32:13. Moses asked God to spare his people the fury of his wrath. God then asked for ten men from among the people as he had done in Sodom.

Moses: Well, there's me, Aaron, Eleazar, and Ithamar, Phinehas, and Caleb, and Joshua.

God: "That's only seven. Where are the other three?"

A little muddled, Moses says, "O Eternal Spirit, (הם חיים המתים) do those who are dead, go on living in you?

God "Yes"

Moses: If those that are dead do live, count Abraham, Isaac, and Jacob also.

Note: Josephus (a sham historian and Roman conspirator who is likely to have corrupted much of the Canonical Gospels) made similar references to this passage. The notion of an afterlife, however desirable, is irrelevant to the intrinsic value of the Kingdom teachings. Taken as allegory however, this passage is a powerful reminder of being made whole (complete) through a oneness with the Spirit.

After this, the very scribes who rehearsed the scriptures by rote were bewildered by Jesus' depth and clarity of understanding...

Scribes: Teacher, you have spoken well.

Jesus offered them unsolicited food for thought....

Jesus: In what sense do they say that the Christ will be David's son? For David himself says in the book of Psalms, 'The Lord said to my Lord, "Sit at my right hand…" If David then, calls Him "Lord" how can he be called his son?"

In this particular passage, the Gospels have Jesus referencing the prophecies of Isaiah? 11:1-9

"And there shall come forth a rod out of the stem of Jesse, and a branch shall grow out of his roots: and the spirit of the LORD shall rest upon him, the spirit of wisdom and understanding, the spirit of counsel and might, the spirit of knowledge and of the fear of the LORD; And shall make him of quick understanding in the fear of the LORD: and he shall not judge after the sight of his eyes, neither reprove after the hearing of his ears: But with righteousness shall he judge the poor, and reprove with equity for the meek of the earth: and he shall smite the earth with the rod of his mouth, and with the breath of his lips shall he slay the wicked. And righteousness shall be the girdle of his loins, and faithfulness the girdle of his reins. The wolf also shall dwell with the lamb, and the leopard shall lie down with the kid; and the calf and the young lion and the fatling together; and a little child shall lead them. And the cow and the bear shall feed; their young ones shall lie down together: and the lion shall eat straw like the ox. And the sucking child shall play on the hole of the asp, and the weaned child shall put his hand on the cockatrice' den. They shall not hurt nor destroy in all my holy mountain: for the earth shall be full of the knowledge of the LORD, as the waters cover the sea."

Was Jesus saying that he was the branch from David's root (Alpha and Omega) that would renew God's peaceful Kingdom after which, even the lion would lay with the lamb? (inhale...) Many religionists today would probably agree with that interpretation. But, as Jesus' follow-up statements seem to warn us, the scribes who were (responsible for reciting and copying Biblical scripture by hand) made profitable errors.

Within earshot of all people listening, Jesus turned to his disciples and spoke...

Jesus: "Beware of the scribes, who like walking around in long robes and who love greetings in the marketplaces and the best seats in the synagogues and the places of honor at banquets, who devour the houses of widows and pray lengthy prayers for the sake of appearance for they are severely condemned!"

Religionists: You convict yourself! The prophets died. So did Abraham, yet you say that he who fulfills your teaching will receive life eternal.

Jesus: Moses commanded you to circumcise your sons. But it wasn't the Spirit who gave Moses this command. It was the customs of your ancestors, and yet even on the Sabbath you circumcise your sons. [You break the laws of Moses in order to the customs of your people.] Why then, are you angry with me for making someone whole on the Sabbath? Don't judge according to appearances but by what is right.

Some of the people from Jerusalem whispered among themselves...

"Isn't this the man they want to kill? Yet here he is, speaking for everyone to hear. And no one is arguing with him. Do you suppose the authorities know that he is the Messiah? But how could that be? No one knows where the Messiah will come from, but we know where this man comes from."

Jesus heard the people and knew that they did not understand the philosophical significance of his teachings, and still sought proofs.

Jesus: Do you really think it's of any consequence that you know me and from where I came? I do not teach of my own accord but in the Spirit of Truth. But you do not recognize it because you are bound by fear and doubt. But when you know the truth, it will set you free.

Those who truly sought righteousness said, "What this man says is inspired by God!" Those who valued the illusory trappings of this world, sought further proof in the prophecies and the working of miracles. The religionist teachers sent emissaries to entrap Jesus and dispute his teachings. But they all returned saying, "We can do nothing with him." Those who speak the truth feel no need to put on false airs pretending to work miracles as proof of their teachings. Jesus simply taught what he believed to be true, risking his life in the process.

Chief priest: How is it you have not convicted him?

Religionist Officials: No one ever spoke as he does. It signifies nothing that you cannot refute him and that the people believe his teaching. We do not believe it and none of the rulers believe it. The people are accursed, they always were stupid and ignorant, and will believe anyone.

Nicodemus: A man should not be condemned without being heard, and without understanding what he teaches.

Chief priest: There is nothing to hear or to understand. We know that no prophet can come from Galilee.

Remember the confusion amongst the disciples in Mark 10:35-45 who were upset with James and John (the sons of Zebedee). Well, there is disagreement amongst the gospels as to when this conflict actually occurred and who it was that actually asked for the favor. According to Matthew 20:20 it was somewhere in this area of the timeline and it was actually James and John's mother, Salome who asked Jesus if her sons could sit on the right and left of Jesus throne in Heaven. Whoever it was who made the request obviously misunderstood the egalitarian nature of the Kingdom. Jesus sat the disciples down and explained that in the world of Men, they appoint governors to serve as rulers over them. Those sovereigns inevitably put their power on display and abuse it for their own devises. But this is not the way of the Kingdom. If any man desires to lead, they shall put themselves last. Jesus told his would be followers to relinquish their old lives and follow him on the spot. But He did not wish to be called "master or even "good." His only concern was to advance the Kingdom. And he gave his life freely to set an example.

Jesus reminded his disciples of the parable of the vineyard workers. (The last were paid first and the first were paid last.) He told them what he had said to the pompous guests who took the most honored places at the wealthy religionist's table. And then he reminded them of the three parables of the "lost"...

Parable 1. Which of you, having a 100 sheep and losing one, would not leave the 99 in the field and search for the lost one? You would go and search until you find it. And when you do find it, you will rejoice greatly. You will carry it home and go to your friends and neighbors saying, "Be happy with me because I found my lost sheep!" In the same way, I tell you the Kingdom of heaven is most joyful when the lost are found. There is more joy for that one sinner than for 99 who don't feel the need to change…

Parable 2: "Suppose a woman has ten silver coins, but she loses one of them. She will take a light and clean the whole house. She will look carefully for the coin until she finds it. And when does, she will call her friends and neighbors and saying, "Rejoice with me because I have found the coin that I lost!"

In the same way, it's a happy time for the children of God when one of their lost is found…

Parable 3: There was a man who had two sons. The younger boy said to his father, "Give me now the part of your property that I am supposed to receive someday." So the father divided his wealth between his two sons. A few days later, the younger son gathered up all that he had and left. He traveled far away to another country, and there he squandered his money and lived like a fool. After he had spent all that he had, there was a terrible famine throughout the country. He was hungry and needed money. So he went and got a job with one of the people who lived there. The man sent him into the fields to feed pigs. He was so hungry that he wanted to eat the food the pigs were eating. But no one gave him anything. Realizing the errors of his ways, he thought, "All my father's hired workers have plenty of food. But here I am, almost dead because I have nothing to eat. I will return to my father's house. I am no longer worthy to be called his son but maybe he will let me be as one of his hired workers." So the once prodigal son went and returned to his father. While the son was still a long way off, his father saw him coming and felt sorry for him. So he ran to him and hugged and kissed him. The son said, "Father, I have sinned against God and have done wrong to you. I am no longer worthy to be called your son." But the father said to his servants, "Hurry! **Jesus Continues:** Bring the best clothes and put them on him. Also, put a ring on his finger and good sandals on his feet. My son was dead, but now he is alive again! He was lost, but now he is found!" So they began to have a party. Now, the older son had been out in the field. When he came near the house, he heard the sound of music and dancing. So he called to one of the servant boys and asked, "What is the meaning of all this?" The boy said, "Your brother has come back, and your father is happy because he has his son back safe and sound." The older son was angry and would not join in the festivities. So his father went out and begged him to come in. But he said to his father, "Look, for all these years I have worked like a slave for you. I have always done what you told me to do, and you never gave me even a young goat for a party with my friends. But then this son of yours comes home after wasting your money on prostitutes, and you hold a great feast for him!" His father said to him, "Oh, my son, you are always with me, and everything I have is yours. But this is a day to be happy and celebrate. Your brother was dead, but now he is alive. He was lost, but now he is found.

Jesus wanted his followers to understand that their true birthright is to serve a purpose greater than themselves. Lest they squander it on the illusive promises of this inequitable realm.

The book of Mark [11:28-12:12] reports of one occasion where Jesus was walking around in the temple in Jerusalem when the senior priests, scribes and the elders confronted him openly...

Religionists: By what authority do you teach? And who gave you this permission to do them here?"

Jesus: Answer me this one thing and I will tell you by what authority I teach... John the Baptist's teachings – was it from Heaven, or from men? Answer me that."

The highbrow religionists reasoned among themselves saying, "If we should say, "From heaven," he will say, "Why do you not believe in me also?" (The people believe that John was a great prophet.) Should we say, "of men" they will surely lose their faith in us.

Religionists: "We do not know."

Jesus: Neither do I tell you by what authority I do these things."

Jesus' gave this response on more than one occasion.[Mat_21:27; Mar_11:33; Luk_20:8] perhaps as an illustration of Proverbs 26:4, "Answer not a fool according to his folly, lest thou also be like unto him." No good can come from resisting evil with evil.

Jesus taught his followers that though they will be rejected by the Orthodox Church, they will be ratified as the cornerstones of the Kingdom...

Jesus: "A man planted a vineyard and put a fence round it. He dug a vat pit and built a tower. Then, he hired laborers, gave them authority over it and went into a far Kingdom In due time, he sent a servant to the husbandmen, in order to observe the fruits of their labors. But they took him and flogged him and sent him off empty-handed. Then he sent another servant to them. But they stoned that one and beat him on the head and sent him off having been shamefully treated. Then he sent another one. But they killed that one, and many others, flogging some and killing others. Well then, still having his one son, his beloved, he also sent him, the last one, to them, and said, 'They will respect my son.' But those farmers said to themselves, 'This is the heir. Come on, let's kill him, and the inheritance will be ours.' So they took him and killed him and disposed of him outside the vineyard. What, then, will the lord of the vineyard do? He will come and destroy the farmers and give the vineyard to others. And have you not read this scripture, 'The stone which the builders rejected is what has become the keystone.

The religionists were as the murderous husbandmen in Jesus' parable who sought even harder for a way to seize him. But because they feared the crowd, they left him and departed.

Darkness wanes in the Presence of Light.

We are no better than the commercialist religionist who divert what is God's (people's desire for love and truth) to our own devices. We could continue to serve our individualistic egos (look where that's gotten us) or we can choose to speak to the truth. What greater legacy than to preserve for our children, their natural right to life? There is a war afoot, but the evils of this world cannot be fought by evil means.

Both Matthew 26:36 and Mark 14:32 record that Jesus was troubled by, Peter's vow to die alongside him for many would die proudly for the glory of Men but few as a testimony against it. As great a love as this, is the least of what is required for to advance the Kingdom of Heaven on earth. Jesus wanted his followers to be so filled with the spirit of compassion that they would gladly give of their lives rather than to risk harm to their assailants in their resistance.

Jesus' knew that his disciples would abandon him because he knew that they were not prepared to relinquish their lives for the sake of love rather than glory as would most men do. To strengthen their faith, he asked them to pray with him in the Garden of Gethsemane. But because they kept falling asleep (failed weigh the costs) they were not prepared for the tribulations that would come.

Disciples, You say that we must love without fail. Increase our faith so that we may believe more firmly in the ways of the Kingdom.

Jesus, It is like a single grain of mustard seed, which a man took and threw in his own garden, and it grew and became a tree so great that the birds of the heavens nestled in its branches."

He possessed the faith of a servant, not of magi...

Jesus, Would a servant coming in from the field after plowing or keeping sheep expect his master to say, "'Come at once and recline at the table?" Or would he rather expect his master to say "Prepare supper for me, and dress properly to serve me while I eat and drink. Then you may serve yourself." Does the servant expect thanks because he performed as expected of him? We have the privilege of serving a cause, the effects of which extend far beyond the limits or our own lives. We should therefore be as humble servants thinking gratefully, "I have done nothing deserving of praise for my service to the Kingdom has been both an honor and a pleasure. It is the purpose for which I was created."

Even as the days of Noah and Lot

Along the way to Jerusalem (somewhere between Samaria and Galilee) Jesus was approached by some religionists asking when the Kingdom of God would come...

Jesus: "The Kingdom of God does not come in ways that can be observed. For no one will say, 'look, it is here" or "it is over there" for the Kingdom of God is in already amidst you."

Jesus turned to his disciples...

Jesus: The day will come when people look for signs but they will not see it. And they will say to you, "Look over there!" or "Look over here!" But do not go out or follow them. For as the lightning flashes and lights up the sky from one side to the other, so is the Kingdom of God.

Jesus told his followers that Heaven is not as people imagine it: some distant place in the far off space. Rather, the Kingdom is in the midst of us. Luke 10:9-11; Matthew 12:28; John 1:26 Jesus compared it to the story of Noah. People ate and drank as if nothing were awry. They married and were given in marriage, even until the day when Noah entered the ark. The proverbial floods came down all around them, but because of their insolence, they paid them no head...

And What Would a Man Give?

There is a thin line between the use of allegory for the purpose of attaining insight and the insane conjectures of all out mysticism. But Jesus often presented these parallels to show that people pay no heed to signs. In this instance, he transitions from the story of Noah to the story of Lot. In both cases people were eating, drinking, buying, selling, planting and building right up to the day when Noah boarded the vessel and Lot walked out of Sodom. In Noah's case it was rain that fell from the sky and destroyed them all. In the story of lot, it was fire and sulfur. "But to whom the Kingdom of Heaven is revealed" will have no concern for the iniquitous riches and illusory pleasures of this world. Ever watchful, the children of the Kingdom will not come down from the rooftop to remove their possessions from their homes. The "one who is in the field will not look back" for there is nothing of this world they wish to retain.

Jesus: Remember Lot's wife and when I said "If anyone would come after me, let him deny himself and take up his cross and follow me. For whoever would save his life will lose it, but whoever loses his life for the sake of the Kingdom will save it. For what does it profit a man to gain the whole world and forfeit himself in the process? And what would a man give in exchange for his soul?

Gandhi. The golden rule is resolutely to refuse to have what the millions cannot. This ability to refuse will not descend upon us all of a sudden. The first thing is to cultivate the mental attitude that will not have possessions or facilities denied to millions, and the next immediate thing is to re-arrange our lives as fast as possible in accordance with that mentality.

Gandhi believed that the path to wholeness requires the heart of a humble servant. That is, in order to truly follow the will of the spirit, one must relinquish everything that stands between them.

Gandhi. Love and exclusive possession can never go together. Theoretically, where there is perfect love, there must be perfect non-possession. The body is our last possession. So, a man can only exercise perfect love and be completely dispossessed if he is prepared to embrace death and renounce his body for the sake of human service. But that is true in theory only. In actual life we can hardly exercise perfect love, for the body as possession will always remain imperfect and it will always be his part to try to be perfect. So that perfection in love or non-possession will remain an unattainable ideal as long as we are alive, but towards which we must ceaselessly strive.

One need only look at the world through the eyes of a child to see the Kingdom. Sadly, after being indoctrinated into the world however, we lose our way. But Jesus indicated that this is for now, part of the human experience. Jesus was grieved to learn that his disciples had been turning children away from him. He calls for one of them and picked him up in his arms and spoke...

Jesus: Whosoever shall humble himself as this little child, the same will be exalted in the Kingdom of Heaven. And whoever receives such a person (as they are) receives me also. But it would be better for him that would corrupt one of these little ones (indoctrinating them to the ways of this world) if he were to have a millstone hanged about his neck and drowned in the depth of the sea. The miseries of this world are brought about because of these offences! It is necessary that these tribulations should come but I grieve for the person who perpetuates them.

It is at this point that Jesus stresses the importance of sanctity concerning the minds of children.

Jesus: If your hand or your foot makes you sin, cut it off and throw it away. It is better for you to lose part of your body and have eternal life than to have your whole body be tossed into the funeral pyre.

Jesus Continues: If your eye makes you sin, then pluck it out and throw it away also. It is better for you to have only one eye and have eternal life than to have two eyes and be thrown into the valley of Ge-Hinnom. Take heed that ye despise not one of these little ones. Consider this: if a man has a hundred sheep, and one of them goes astray, does he not leave the other ninety-nine, and go into the mountains, and search of the one gone astray? And if so be that he find it, verily I say unto you, he rejoices more of that sheep, than of the ninety-nine which went not astray. Even so it is not the will of your Father which is in heaven, that one of these little ones should be lost.

We come into this world with the light of the Kingdom shining forth from within our hearts. But then we are taught to be unjust with one another; to strike first and hardest and to take more than is needed lest we put ourselves at the mercy of others. We teach our children to wear expensive clothes and to use material possessions as outward signs of personal substance. Of course these notions are far too absurd to be conveyed outright. Rather, they are inferred by example. But Jesus said that one would be better to have a millstone hanged about his neck and drowned in the depth of the sea than to corrupt the mind of a child in this way.

Like most people, I long for God most in times of trouble or feel the least self-capable. As a psychologist, I was trained to treat such "low self-esteem" as one treats a mental disorder. Without such "dis-ease" however, the disparity of this realm would go amiss. Psychology isn't the cure anymore than religion. Neither should one's spiritual (psychosocial) endeavors be motivated by a need to building oneself up. Rather, it should involve a process of tearing down the walls between oneself and the Spirit of God; however you choose to define it (truth, love, empathy, compassion, oneness, etc.).

Our civilization, our culture, our Swaraj depend not upon multiplying our wants--self-indulgence, but upon restricting our wants--self-denial.

--Gandhi

Gandhi said that Jesus, Mahomed, Buddha, Nanak, Kabir, Chaitanya, Shankara, Dayanand, Ramakrishna were all "men who exercised an immense influence over and molded the character of thousands of men." The "world is the richer" wrote Gandhi, "for their having lived in it." Gandhi made a point to mention that each of these men "deliberately embraced poverty" as an integral provision of their journey and that people are spiritually demoralized to the extent that they embrace the "modern materialistic craze."

How heavy is the toll of sins and wrongs that wealth, power and prestige exact from man!

-Gandhi

Gandhi defined theft simply as taking something from another without permission. He explained that, "to use a thing for a purpose different from the one intended by the lender or to use it for a period longer than that which has been fixed with him" is also theft. Gandhi believed it a "profound truth" that everything has a purpose, and its creation is limited to that which is strictly needed to fulfil it. Therefore, whoever appropriates more than is minimally necessary for sustenance, while others have less than they need is also guilty of thievery.

Renounce all and dedicate it to God and then live. The right of living is thus derived from renunciation. It does not say, 'When all do their part of the work, I too will do it.' It says, 'Don't bother about others, do your job first and leave the rest to Him.

-Gandhi

Jesus said that we shouldn't worry for what we will eat or drink, for God will supply our needs. Gandhi considered this, the secret to happiness...

Gandhi. The secret of happy life lies in renunciation. Renunciation is life. Indulgence spells death. Therefore, everyone has a right and should desire to live 125 years while performing service without an eye on result. Such life must be wholly and solely dedicated to service. Renunciation made for the sake of such service is an ineffable joy of which none can deprive one, because that nectar springs from within and sustains life. In this there can be no room for worry or impatience. Without this joy, long life is impossible and would not be worthwhile even if possible.

The Great Salt March

We are all Children of God

When a fox is caught in a trap, it will gnaw off its own leg in defense of its life. That is how we should view the alluring snares of this world. The darkest most inescapable purgatory is within one's own vindictive heart. It is rightly said, that the opposite of love is not hate, but indifference.

Jesus: Remember the parable of the lost sheep? If your brother or sister does something wrong, go and make peace with them.

Peter: When someone does me wrong, how many times must I forgive them? Is seven times enough?"

Jesus: I tell you, you must forgive them more than seven times. You must continue to forgive them even if they wrong you seventy times seven."

It is important to note that Jesus, in no way, restricted forgiveness. The emphasis on the number seven (the factor of Enlightenment) is a simply reference of Buddhist derivative meant to imply perfection. Jesus' doctrine of non-resistance is founded on the premise that sin is a "dis-ease" caused by a perceived disunion between one's self and another. The only remedy for sin is unrelenting mercy. It is for this reason that Jesus taught his followers to forgive without fail.

The Mercy Paradox

People tend to rationalize immoral behavior as retribution for past wrongs. "Sin," is therefore perpetuated from an unwillingness to forgive the perceived trespasses of another. How then, can one pray for absolution from sin without first absolving themselves from the snares of animosity?

Jesus: The way of the kingdom may be compared to a king who wanted to settle accounts with his subjects. One of them owed him several thousand pounds of silver but was unable to pay. So the master ordered the debtor and all his possessions to be sold along with his wife and children. The money would be used to pay the king the man's debts. But the debtor fell on his knees and begged saying, "Be patient with me. I will pay you everything I owe." The master felt sorry for the man and released him from his debt. "Later, that same servant confronted a man who owed him a hundred silver coins. He grabbed his debtor by the throat saying, 'Pay me the money you owe me!' The second debtor fell on his knees and begged as the first had done saying, "Be patient with me. I will pay you everything I owe." But the first debtor refused to be patient. He took him to the judge and had him thrown in jail until he could pay everything he owed. The other subjects, seeing what had happened felt sorry for the second debtor. They went to their master and told him everything that had happened. Then the master called his servant in and said, "You evil servant. You begged me to forgive your debt, and I forgave them all! So you should have shown your debtors the same mercy and forgiven them their debts also." The master was very angry, so he put the servant in jail to be punished. And he had to stay in jail until he could pay everything he owed.

In the meantime, the chief priests gathered together to decide what they should do to end Jesus' disruptive influence once and for all. Though the chief religionist assembled in secret, it isn't hard to imagine the dialogue as it is would transpire even today:

"The public is obviously too naive to think for themselves. This man teaches that all Men are created equal and are of children of one nation under God!"

"And what would come of our people should they subscribe to his doctrine of peaceful protest? The enemy will overwhelm us and the traditions of our forefathers will be for naught."

"How can we arrest him in secret and silence him
before any more believe in his ridiculous "Kingdom"
movement? If we do not act soon, the Roman
government will step in and we will lose what rights we
have left."

Of course, some among them would have been moved by their conscience saying, "this man has done nothing wrong!" The authors of the Gospels indicate that even the most righteous among them were overcome with intimidation as the high priest thundered over them:

Caiaphas: You just don't get it! How can you not see that
it is more profitable for one man to die than for the whole
Hebrew Nation to perish?"

From that day forward the religionist resolved that Jesus should be publicly shamed and executed in disgrace. Meanwhile Jesus was leaving the temple courts. His disciples were in awe of how its gold trimmed marble buildings shimmered like snow in the sunset. But Jesus was not impressed...

Jesus: You see all these great buildings? There shall not
be one stone left upon another that shall not be thrown
down!

Spy Wednesday

Jesus spends the evening in Bethany, a little village near the Mt. of Olives which is very close to Jerusalem. While there, he was received into the home of Simon who suffered from leprosy, Mary (Magdalene) and her sister Martha. Mary sits at the feet of Jesus and listens attentively as he ministers on the Kingdom. Martha however, felt unfairly encumbered by the chores of hosting.

Disciple: What a waist. That could have been sold for a great sum and given to the poor!

Jesus: Do not discourage her! For, you do not know what manner of spirit is upon you. The poor have always been with us and you could have given money to them anytime you wanted. But now that this woman wishes to humble herself before me, you wish bring them up. You can be sure that some here today will speak fondly of her, and they will tell others the world over. Wherever the "Good News" is told, she will be remembered.

Jesus tells Mary that though she has fulfilled the urging of the Spirit, she should reserve the oil to anoint his body for the day of his burial. Upon hearing this, Mary cries and uses her hair to wipe her tears from Jesus' feet. Martha gasps...

Martha: "Doesn't it bother you that my sister has left me to serve alone? Will you please tell her to come and help me?"

Jesus: Martha, thou art careful and troubled about many things. But only one is important. Mary has chosen that better part, which shall not be taken away from her.

Note: The authors of the canonical gospels hold very different opinions of this woman who came to Jesus carrying an alabaster box filled with oil. One contributor of Luke 7:37 presents her early on in Jesus' ministry as a sinner whom...

"...stood at his feet behind him weeping, and began to wash his feet with tears, and did wipe them with the hairs of her head, and kissed his feet, and anointed them with the ointment."

No wonder the self-righteous host acted with indignation (See also, pgs. 135 & 301). An author of Matthew 26:7 says that she broke the seal of an alabaster box of very precious ointment, and "poured it on his head..." and least one contributor to the gospel of Mark14:3 concedes. Obviously, the gospel authors had different political aims for presenting Mary in such dissimilar ways. The apparent goal of the immediate passage however, is to present Jesus as the ultimate sacrifice for humanity's moral turpitude.

The proponents of commercial religion divert what is God's for their own devices. "Just believe that God gave his only son" as payment (along with your tithes) for your continued sin and be absolved of it. Mysticism is another name for commercial religion. The books in this Rational Bible series have shown that much if not all of the Bible's happenings originated as pure allegory. In one passage, a particular event is presented as historical fact. In another, it is a parable presented by Jesus. Somewhere along the line, early evangelists simply became more interested in deifying the central figure of the Christian faith than in advancing the philosophy behind it.

The objective of this book however, is simply to present a functional amalgamation of the Gospels in hopes of resurfacing the original Kingdom teachings. Should the reader wish to further include Mary Magdalene in their personal rendition, they might note that in the book of John she comes to the tomb alone before the sun came up. The idea that she reserved the precious oil to anoint Jesus' body also flows nicely with Mark's 16:1 rendering that Mary was one of the women who came early Sunday morning to Jesus' tomb to anoint his body. What doesn't mesh however, is the utterly irrational and inconsistent claim that Jesus raised her brother Lazarus (or himself for that matter) from the dead. Interestingly, Jesus' own parable Luke 16:19-31 featuring Lazarus himself, refutes this...

Jesus: There was a certain rich man, which was clothed in purple and fine linen, and fared sumptuously every day. And there was a certain beggar named Lazarus, which was laid at his gate, full of sores, And desiring to be fed with the crumbs which fell from the rich man's table; moreover the dogs came and licked his sores. **And it came to pass, that the beggar died,** and was carried by the angels into Abraham's bosom; **the rich man also died,** and was buried; And in hell he lift up his eyes, being in torments, and seeth Abraham afar off, and Lazarus in his bosom. And he cried and said, Father Abraham, have mercy on me, and send Lazarus, that he may dip the tip of his finger in water, and cool my tongue; for I am tormented in this flame. But Abraham said, Son, remember that thou in thy lifetime receivedst thy good things, and likewise Lazarus evil things; but now he is comforted, and thou art tormented. And beside all this, between us and you there is a great gulf fixed; so that they which would pass from hence to you cannot; neither can they pass to us, that would come from thence. Then he said, **I pray thee therefore, father, that thou wouldest send him to my father's house; For I have five brethren; that he may testify unto them, lest they also come into this place of torment.** Abraham saith unto him, **They have Moses and the prophets; let them hear them.** And he said, Nay, father Abraham, **but if one went unto them from the dead, they will repent.** And he said unto him, **If they hear not Moses and the prophets, neither will they be persuaded, though one rose from the dead.** "

Jesus conclusively presented a parable <u>against resurrection</u> as a basis for increasing one's faith. Case closed! Just to demonstrate the lunacy of getting caught up in the study of mysticism, I would like to point out a famous passage in Mark: 14:43-55

"And immediately, while he yet spake, cometh Judas, one of the twelve, and with him a great multitude with swords and staves, from the chief priests and the scribes and the elders. And he that betrayed him had given them a token, saying, Whomsoever I shall kiss, that same is he; take him, and lead him away safely. And as soon as he was come, he goeth straightway to him, and saith, Master, master; and kissed him. And they laid their hands on him, and took him. And one of them that stood by drew a sword, and smote a servant of the high priest, and cut off his ear. And Jesus answered and said unto them, Are ye come out, as against a thief, with swords and with staves to take me? I was daily with you in the temple teaching, and ye took me not: but the scriptures must be fulfilled. And they all forsook him, and fled. And **there followed him a certain young man, having a linen cloth cast about his naked body;** and the young men laid hold on him: And **he left the linen cloth,** and fled from them **naked.** And they led Jesus away to the high priest: and with him were assembled all the chief priests and the elders and the scribes. And Peter followed him afar off, even into the palace of the high priest: and he sat with the servants, and warmed himself at the fire. And the chief priests and all the council sought for witness against Jesus to put him to death; and found none."

We discussed the NT author's intentions behind making Judas a traitor as well as the significance of the silver in the "Rational Bible." John 12:5 actually identifies the person who complained about Mary (see also pgs. 135 & 297) as wasting the precious oil in Mark 14:5 as Judas Iscariot, Simon's son who actually knew the value of the oil as "three hundred pence."

Here's again is Mark's account...

"And being in Bethany in the house of Simon the leper, as he sat at meat, there came a woman having an alabaster box of ointment of spikenard very precious; and she brake the box, and poured it on his head. And there were some that had indignation within themselves, and said, why was this waste of the ointment made? For it might have been sold for more than three hundred pence, and have been given to the poor. And they murmured against her. And Jesus said, Let her alone; why trouble ye her? she hath wrought a good work on me. For ye have the poor with you always, and whensoever ye will ye may do them good: but me ye have not always."

–Mark 14:3–7

And here's John's...

"Then Jesus six days before the passover came to Bethany, where Lazarus was which had been dead, whom he raised from the dead. There they made him a supper; and Martha served; but Lazarus was one of them that sat at the table with him. Then took Mary a pound of ointment of spikenard, very costly, and anointed the feet of Jesus, and wiped his feet with her hair; and the house was filled with the odour of the ointment. Then saith **one of his disciples, Judas Iscariot, Simon's son, which should betray him, Why was not this ointment sold for three hundred pence,** and given to the poor? This he said, not that he cared for the poor; but **because he was a thief, and had the bag, and bare what was put therein.** Then said Jesus, Let her alone; against the day of my burying hath she kept this. For the poor always ye have with you; but me ye have not always.

-John12:1-8

The authors of John go out of their way to depict Judas as a greedy disciple/accountant and that he stole from their purse! The author of John returns to this theme of making Judas a greedy traitor again in chapter 13 verses 23-31. Only this time, Judas is possessed of the devil <u>that Jesus put in him</u>!

"Now there was leaning on Jesus' bosom one of his disciples, **whom Jesus loved**. Simon Peter therefore beckoned to him, that he should ask who it should be of whom he spake. He then lying on Jesus' breast saith unto him, Lord, who is it? Jesus answered, He it is, to whom **I shall give a sop**, when I have dipped it. And when **he had dipped the sop, he gave it to Judas Iscariot, the son of Simon. And after the sop Satan entered into him.** Then said Jesus unto him, That thou doest, do quickly. Now no man at the table knew for what intent he spake this unto him. For some of them thought, **because Judas had the bag**, that Jesus had said unto him, Buy those things that we have need of against the feast; or, that he should give something to the poor. He **then having received the sop** went immediately out: and it was night. Therefore, when he was gone out, Jesus said, Now is the Son of man glorified, and God is glorified in him."

Nothing about this particular account sits well with the astute reader. Maybe that's why the gospel of John was never truly canonized. What personal agenda or political goal was the author trying to accomplish anyway? The outlandish claim that Judas stole from the disciple's purse without anyone noticing actually suggests that the disciples were quite wealthy! This goes against everything Jesus himself taught. By giving Judas the last name "Iscariot," the original author of

Matthew wanted to identify him as an overzealous member of a warrior sect who wished to kindle the fury of Jesus' followers against their Roman oppressors. While slithering down John's rabbit hole, one can't help but wonder "just who is this "disciple whom Jesus loved?"

Well, we know it wasn't Peter (Jesus' rock)...

Therefore that disciple whom Jesus loved saith unto Peter, It is the Lord. Now when Simon Peter heard that it was the Lord, he girt his fisher's coat unto him, (for he was naked,) and did cast himself into the sea.

-John 21:7

Thankfully John narrowed it down to one of three choices

"Now Jesus loved Martha, and her sister, and Lazarus."

-John 11:5

And it could not have been Mary...

The first day of the week cometh Mary Magdalene early, when it was yet dark, unto the sepulchre, and seeth the stone taken away from the sepulchre. Then she runneth, and cometh to Simon Peter, and to the other disciple, whom Jesus loved, and saith unto them, They have taken away the Lord out of the sepulchre, and we know not where they have laid him.

–John 20:1-2

Could there be a gospel of Lazarus?

Well, to answer that question lets go all the way back to the 13th chapter of Mark 11-16:

"But when they shall lead you, and deliver you up, take no thought beforehand what ye shall speak, neither do ye premeditate: but whatsoever shall be given you in that hour, that speak ye: for it is not ye that speak, but the Holy Ghost. **Now the brother shall betray the brother to death,** and the father the son; and children shall rise up against their parents, and shall cause them to be put to death. **And ye shall be hated** of all men for my name's sake: but he that shall endure unto the end, the same shall be saved. But when ye shall see the abomination of desolation, spoken of by Daniel the prophet, standing where it ought not, (let him that readeth understand,) then **let them that be in Judaea flee to the mountains:** And let him that is on the housetop not go down into the house, neither enter therein, to take any thing out of his house: **And let him that is in the field not turn back again for to take up his garment.**

Ah, suddenly Judah's betrayal ^{Mark 14:43-55} and not turning back to retreive one's linen cloth makes sense...

"And he that betrayed him had given them a token, saying, Whomsoever I shall kiss, that same is he... he goeth straightway to him, and saith, Master, master; and kissed him. And they laid their hands on him, and took him. And one of them that stood by drew a sword... And they all forsook him, and fled. And there followed him a certain young man, having a linen cloth cast about his naked body; and the young men laid hold on him. And he left the linen cloth, and fled from them naked. And they led Jesus away to the high priest..."

So why go through all the trouble of making a mystery surrounding "certain" naked man? Perhaps the authors of John needed a 13th disciple!

Again, the authors of Mark obviously wanted to link 14:43-54 back to a passage in the preceding chapter. ^{13:11-16} The authors of John however, had a completely different intention. Hold on to your seat for this one, it's a whopper! Remember, John having written the gospel over a hundred years after Jesus' death never claimed to have been the disciple under his own namesake.

"Then Peter, turning about, **seeth the disciple whom Jesus loved following;** which also leaned on his breast at supper, and said, Lord, which is he that betrayeth thee? **Peter seeing him saith to Jesus, Lord, and what shall this man do?** Jesus saith unto him, **If I will that he tarry till I come, what is that to thee?** follow thou me. Then went this saying abroad among the brethren, that **that disciple should not die** yet **Jesus said not unto him, He shall not die; but, If I will that he tarry till I come, what is that to thee?** *This is the disciple which testifieth of these things, and wrote these things* and we know that his testimony is true. And there are also many other things which Jesus did, the which, if they should be written every one, I suppose that even the world itself could not contain the books that should be written. Amen. "

–John 21:20–25

So there you have it. The authors of John were trying to prove that this "certain young man having a linen cloth cast about his naked body" was Lazarus because they needed to an immortal disciple! Who better than one raised from the dead? Then again, that's an even better reason for why the gospel of John was never canonized.

"And further, by these, my son, be admonished: of making many books there is no end; and much study is a weariness of the flesh."

–Ecclesiastes 12.12

Obviously, the Gospels are the result of thousands of years' worth of editing wars between religious sects, each one having their own political agenda. But the amazing insights which have amassed amidst the irrational muck of absurdity is the result of this ancient but evolutionary form of creative writing. The Bible truly is a living document. At least it was until the advent of the printing press. But the "Word" doesn't have to be lost to a perfectly rational humanity. The Latin derivative of the word "religion" is "religaire" which literally means to bind or "tie-back." Perhaps it's time we utilize scriptures minus the hokum of religious fundamentalism? Be sure to contact: media@rationalbible.com if you would like to make suggestions, contribute or inquire about the next edition of the rational bible series. I'm expecting some pretty heavy feedback on this one.

Holy Thursday

On this first day of the "unleavened bread" Jesus' sent his disciples to make preparations for the Passover meal in Jerusalem. Later that evening, he offered the Last Supper. Jesus broke the bread into twelve pieces (as he had done in the wilderness among the 5000) and gave one to each of them. Then he filled a cup with wine from which they each drank in communion.

Assumed the role of humble servant, Jesus then took a pitcher of water, poured it out into a basin and began washing each of the disciple's feet.

Jesus: As I mentioned, one of you will betray me and my blood will be shed. Even so, I have fed him, given him drink and washed his feet. In this way, you too should treat those who would betray you.

Note: It is safe to assume that Judas, having remorse, forewarned Jesus of his betrayal but Jesus did not resist even this transgression against him. The disciples began to ask Jesus which of them was the traitor. But Jesus, showing mercy, would not endanger Judas either to the high priests or his fellow disciples. When it grew dark, Jesus signaled Judas in secret, to go and complete his mission.

Jesus: This is what it means to serve the Kingdom. To truly worship God, we must love one another as he loves us. A father doesn't love only those children who love him back. In that way, we should love even those who would do us harm. Do not do as the religionists do. Don't argue

about my teachings one praising himself above another.
Refer to my teachings to verify what you already know
within your hearts: that true glory comes not from Men,
but from the Kingdom of God. All the commandments
can be surmised as only this: love they neighbor as
thyself. Do not condemn as the religionist do. The
Kingdom begins within you.

While Jesus and his disciples sang hymns, he began
to suffer the pangs of the flesh. In that moment, he
projected the spirit of fear and trepidation upon them.

Jesus: Each of you will forsake me when they come to
take me.

Peter: No, how could you say such a thing? I would give
my life for you.

The other disciples agreed that they would defend
Jesus till the death. But when Jesus heard the mention
of knives, he became even more weary of the spirit
which had overtaken him.

Jesus asked the disciples to go with him to pray in
the garden of Gethsemane.

Jesus: Go with me and pray for the strength to honor God
even in this darkest hour.

Peter, John and James walked with Jesus. Once in the
garden, Jesus moved "a stone's throw away" them and
fell to his knees in anguish...

Jesus: My Father, if it be possible, let this cup pass from me; nevertheless not as I will, but as thou wilt..

Jesus turned to his disciples and found them asleep. He woke them saying, "What, could ye not watch with me one hour? Watch and pray, that ye enter not into temptation: the spirit indeed *is* willing, but the flesh *is* weak. He returned to pray a second time...

Jesus: Dear Father, if this cup may not pass away from me, except I drink it, thy will be done.

And then Jesus looked and found them asleep again for they were very tired. Luke records that in his agony Jesus tarried the same prayer even more earnestly. So much so that his sweat was like "great drops of blood falling down to the ground." Yet when he returned to his disciples this time he said, "Rise, let us be going: behold, he is at hand that doth betray me. On January 28th, 1948, just two days prior to assassination, Gandhi similarly stated...

"If I am to die by the bullet of a mad man, I must do so smiling. There must be no anger within me. God must be in my heart and on my lips."

Jesus and his disciples exited the Garden. As they entered their encampment, they saw Judas accompanied by Caiaphas' soldiers. Peter drew a knife and prepared to fight...

Jesus: Remember Peter, he who lives by the sword dies by the sword.

In this way, Jesus reminded Peter that to take a life is to sever the sacred. The disciples were prepared to fight and die for the glory of Men. But they were not prepared to give it freely in defiance of it. Rather, they fled the proving ground just as Jesus had predicted. For they had not fully weighed the cost.

Though Jesus went willingly, the commanding officer ordered him bound and taken to Annas (the former high priest who remained in the house of Caiaphas) as a prisoner. Jesus faced 7 agonizing trials. The first of which were convened in secret. He was taken to the house of Caiaphas, the high priest who had intimidated the others saying, "it is better that one man should die, than for the whole of the people to perish." Caiaphas, sought the expertise of Annas, his father in law, on how he should find sufficient cause enough to stifle the moral sense of the less corrupt and intimidated members of the Council. Annas asked Jesus about the nature of his "strange" doctrine. For he did not recognize what was good of the very doctrine for which he himself professed to teach. Jesus subtly addresses the sinister agenda of his religionist captors. For they did not seek to understand but only to condemn.

Jesus: I always answered openly to anyone who asks with a sincere heart. I have taught in the synagogues, the temple or any place where people assemble themselves in public. In secret, I have said nothing.

Jesus continues: Why then, do you ask me here in the darkness on night? If you truly wish to know the gospel of the Kingdom, ask those who have heard me, for they know all that I profess.

When Jesus said this, an officer of the high priest struck him with the palm of his hand.

Offending officer: You will address the high priest will respect?

Jesus turned to his assailant, the cheek which had not been struck...

Jesus: If I have spoken evil, bear witness of the evil. But if I have spoken well, why did you strike me?

Since Annas could not snare Jesus by his words, Caiaphas sought witnesses to testify falsely against him. He had Jesus brought before the counsel of scribes and the elders of the Church. At first, it seemed as though no one could speak ill of him.

After a seemingly endless line of testimonies however, Caiaphas brought two false witnesses.

False Witnesses: This fellow said, "I have the power to destroy the very temple of God, and to rebuild it in three days' time without lifting so much as a finger."

Caiaphas jumped to his feet saying, "Do you not wish to defend yourself against these accusations? Jesus held his peace. He would not resist an evil.

Caiaphas: I command you under the authority of the living God to tell us once and for all whether you consider yourself be the Christ, the Son of God.

Jesus: Those are your words, not mine. Nevertheless, I proudly stand before you, a child of God.

Hearing this, Caiaphas ripped his own clothes in anger...

Caiaphas: What do we need of any further witnesses? You have heard the blasphemy. What do you think?

Those who dared speak, condemned Jesus to death. Someone blindfolded him and they began to spit on Jesus and strike him with their fist and the palms of their hands.

Assailant: Prophesy, who is it that smote thee?

The purpose of the first two trials, for which the religionists apparently succeeded, was to kill the people's faith in the teachings of Jesus. At this point however, the noble intent of each malefactor should be noted. The goal of the chief priests, was to retain their way of life. Jesus' teachings threatened to disrupt the "peace." Judas' did not wish to betray Jesus, but to incite the fury of his large followership against their Roman oppressors. Above all, we should seek to advance the Kingdom of Heaven on earth and leave the rest to God. And if there be no God or Kingdom, then one is better to have forsaken the illusory concerns of this world than to have conceded its unjust conditions.

"Good" Friday

At dawn, the chief priests, elders and scribes reassembled to find dissent among them.

Religionist Officials: Tell us clearly do you consider yourself to be "the Christ?"

Jesus: If I tell you, you will not believe. And if I ask also what you believe, you will not answer, nor let me go. But I am not afraid. You may kill the body, and after that, there is no more that you can do. For then I shall be one with God.

Remembering how Caiaphas had riled the crowd the night before, they rephrased the question...

Religionist Officials: "Okay let me ask you this way, Are you the Son of God?"

Jesus: If that is the way you wish to put it.

Religionist Officials: Why do we need any further witnesses? For again, we ourselves have witnessed the words out of his own mouth.

It was not within the Sanhedrin's authority to condemn a man to death. For this, they would need a Roman governor.

The religionists could not defile themselves before taking Passover. To exact the death penalty on Jesus they would have to rely on the Roman government. Trials in the Roman forum began at daybreak, so they would have to hurry to have Jesus sentenced by the end of the day. When the hypocrites delivered Jesus to Governor Pontius Pilate, they refused to enter the Judgment halls themselves because they had already performed purification ceremonies. Pilate, after finding no fault in Jesus, came out to persuade them of his innocence but the public was now blind to the ruthless exploits of their religious elite. Pilate knew that if he simply let Jesus go, he would be denounced as an insurgent against Caesar (Jesus was accused of claiming kingship). But then Pilate remembered that Jesus (being a Galilean) would fall under Herod Antipas' jurisdiction.

Presented as an act of goodwill toward a long-time enemy, Pilate sent Jesus to Herod who happened to be in Jerusalem for the feast of the Passover. Having heard good things of Jesus' ministry, Herod secretly wished him a long life in continuance of it. He asked Jesus many questions in hopes that he might justify his release, but Jesus refused to answer in his own defense. Other than to face the wrath of the bloodthirsty mob of religionists, Herod had no choice but to have Jesus flogged. He and his soldiers, publicly mocked Jesus, dressing him in a stately robe. After this, Herod sent him back to Pilate where a crown of thorns was thrust upon his head; his body beaten until the robe turned from purple to crimson red.

Religionist Officials: This man is a criminal.

Pilate: What charges do you bring against him?

Religionist Officials: He claims to be the Christ.

Pilate: Then take him and judge him according to your own Law.

Religionist Officials: Under our Laws, he must be put to death. Yet, it is unlawful for us to put any man to death during the Passover. We found this man guilty of stirring up a rebellion. He agitates the people, forbidding his followers from paying tribute to Caesar and even hailing himself as the Christ, the legitimate King of the Jews!

Pilate: Art thou the King of the Jews?

Jesus: Sayest thou this thing of thyself, or did others tell it thee of me?

Pilate: Am I a Jew? Thine own nation and the chief priests have delivered thee unto me: what hast thou done?

Jesus: My kingdom is not of this world: if my kingdom were of this world, then would my servants fight, that I should not be delivered to the (commercial religionists) but now is my kingdom not from hence.

Pilate therefore said unto him, Art thou a king then?

Jesus: Thou sayest that I am a king?

"To this end was I born, and for this cause came I into the world, that I should bear witness unto the truth. Every one that is of the truth heareth my voice."

Pilate: What is truth?

Appendix A: "Q & A with Gandhi"

I found it useful during the initial stages of my research to compile and catalog some of Gandhi's more definitive verbal replies and written observations. In an effort to better understand his philosophy, I took the liberty of presenting them to myself in question and answer format as if interviewing Gandhi in person. A sample of what became *"Conversation with Gandhi"* is as follows:

I understand that you are a student of philosophy. How important is it to "know thyself?"

Gandhi: A man is but the product of his thoughts. What he thinks, he becomes... It is good to see ourselves as others see us. Try as we may, we are never able to know ourselves fully as we are, especially the evil side of us. This we can do only if we are not angry with our critics but will take in good heart whatever they might have to say... The best way to find yourself is to lose yourself in the service of others.

Is there any purpose in which war is justified?

Gandhi: Nonviolence is not a garment to be put on and off at will. Its seat is in the heart, and it must be an inseparable part of our being...What kind of victory is it when someone is left defeated? You must be the change you wish to see in the world... It may be long before the law of love will be recognized in international affairs. The machineries of government stand between and hide the hearts of one people from those of another... Peace will not come out of a clash of arms but out of justice lived and done by unarmed nations in the face of odds.... What does it matter to the dead, the orphans, and the homeless whether the mad destruction   is wrought under the name of totalitarianism or the holy name of liberty or democracy?... Democracy and violence can ill go together. Evolution of democracy is not possible if we are not prepared to hear the other side. Violent means will give violent freedom... However much I may sympathize with and admire worthy motives, I am an uncompromising opponent of violent methods even to serve the noblest of causes

You often speak of a law of love as if it were a force of nature. But it cannot be observed under a microscope much less by human experience. How then do we know it is of any consequence at all?

Gandhi: Love is the strongest force the world possesses... Whether humanity will consciously follow the law of love, I do not know. But that need not disturb me. The law will work just as the law of gravitation works, whether we accept it or not. The person who discovered the law of love was a far greater scientist than any of our modern scientists. Only our explorations have not gone far enough and so it is not possible for everyone to see all its workings.

You say that Non-cooperation with evil is a sacred duty. How exactly does that work?

Gandhi: Nonviolence is the greatest force at the disposal of mankind. It is mightier than the mightiest weapon of destruction devised by the ingenuity of man. Hatred ever kills, love never dies; such is the vast difference between the two. What is obtained by love is retained for all time. What is obtained by hatred proves a burden in reality for it increases hatred... You assist an evil system most effectively by obeying its orders and decrees. An evil system never deserves such allegiance. Allegiance to it means partaking of the evil. A good person will resist an evil system with his or her whole soul...

I've heard that you said "hate the sin but love the sinner." How do you love someone who only causes strife?

Gandhi: Man and his deed are two distinct things. Whereas a good deed should call forth approbation, and a wicked deed disapprobation, the doer of the deed, whether good or wicked always deserves respect or pity as the case may be... The weak can never forgive. Forgiveness is the attribute of the strong... To forgive is not to forget. The merit lies in loving in spite of the vivid knowledge that the one that must be loved is not a friend... Hate the sin and not the sinner is a precept which though easy enough to understand is rarely practiced, and that is why the poison of hatred spreads in the world.

I think the reason so many people fail to turn the other cheek is that they internalize the possibility of being labeled a coward. What are your thoughts on that?

Gandhi: Nonviolence and cowardice are contradictory terms. Nonviolence is the greatest virtue, cowardice the greatest vice. Nonviolence springs from love, cowardice from hate. Nonviolence always suffers, cowardice would always inflict suffering. Perfect nonviolence is the highest bravery. Nonviolent conduct is never demoralizing, cowardice always is... A coward is incapable of exhibiting love; it is the prerogative of the brave

You say that until we lay down our weapons, mankind will never truly be free. But there would be no fear of retribution for harms. In putting down their arms, the good not only forfeit their own lives but the whole world to the vilest of men. Is that no so?

Gandhi: Destruction is not the law of humans. Man lives freely only by his readiness to die, if need be, at the hands of his brother, never by killing him. Every murder or other injury, no matter for what cause, committed or inflicted on another is a crime against humanity.... It is the law of love that rules mankind. Had violence, i.e. hate, ruled us we should have become extinct long ago. And yet, the tragedy of it is that the so-called civilized men and nations conduct themselves as if the basis of society was violence... Man's nature is not essentially evil. Brute nature has been known to yield to the influence of love. You must never despair of human nature... Power is of two kinds. One is obtained by the fear of punishment and the other by acts of love. Power based on love is a thousand times more effective and permanent then the one derived from fear of punishment... Nonviolence is a weapon of the strong

What is your opinion of western civilization?

Gandhi: "I think it would be a good idea."

Now, you had read parts of the Bible before reading Tolstoy's interpretation, am I right?

Gandhi: Yes, while studying for the bar in England, I was given a copy of the New Testament and it went straight to my heart. I tried to read the Old Testament but so much of it did not reconcile with the bidding of returning good for evil. When taken in its whole form, Jesus' Sermon on the Mount is what most endeared me to Christianity.

I heard that during your early days in South Africa you attempted to attend a local Christian Church service. What happened?

Well, when I reached the door, I was blocked by a church elder. He said "Where do you think you are going, kaffir... There is no room for kaffirs in this church. Get out of here or I'll have my assistants throw you down the steps." I was hurt for a while. **Gandhi Continues:** But then I remembered the words of Jesus on the mount saying, "But I say to you, that ye resist not evil: but whosoever smite thee on thy right cheek, turn to him the other also. " Jesus holds a place in my heart as a great teacher of humanity. He has made a considerable influence on my life.

What advice would you give to Christians?"

Christians, especially missionaries, should begin to live more like Christ. You should spread more of the gospel of love and you should study non-Christian faiths to have more sympathetic understanding of their faiths. The most effective way to deliver the gospel is to life it in the beginning, in the middle and in the end. The best form of preaching is a life of service in its uttermost simplicity. But you quote John 3:16 instead

> For God so loved the world, that he gave his only begotten Son, that whosoever believeth in him should not perish, but have everlasting life.

You ask people simply to believe, but empty words have no appeal to me. Wherever there has been acceptance of the gospel through preaching, it is because the motive was already there. A rose does not need to preach. It simply spreads its fragrance. The fragrance IS its own sermon. How we treat others speaks volumes about what we believe.

Gandhi continues: In my youth, my experience with Christian missionaries was less than desirable. They stood on the corner of my grade school loudly mocking the gods and beliefs of Hinduism. New converts to Christianity were "denationalized" and "Britishised." From then on it was "beef and brandy." Many fellow Hindus (mostly vegetarian) considered Christian missionaries, with their overly forceful behavior, to be destroyers of the Indian culture. What is presented as orthodox Christianity is a direct negation of Jesus' Sermon on the Mount. If I could offer only one piece of advice for Christians, it would be to become more Christian.

In your opinion, what do you think went wrong? That is, how did Christianity stray from its Eastern roots and can we get back what was lost?

The message of Jesus of Nazareth, the Son of peace has been little understood in Western world that is steeped in individualistic consumerism and that light upon it may have to be shown from the East. I ask my Christian brethren (in India) do not to accept Christianity as it is interpreted in the West. There, they fight with one another as never before. After all, Jesus was an Asiatic depicted as wearing the Arabian flowing robe. He was the essence of meekness. I hope that the Christians of India will express in their lives Jesus the crucified, of the Bible, and not as interpreted in the West with her blood-stained fingers. I have no desire to criticize the West. I know and value the many virtues of the West. But I am bound to point out that Jesus of Asia is misrepresented in the West except in individuals.

What authenticates the story of Jesus' life for you the most?

Gandhi: Its emphasis on suffering. In fact it, the idea of voluntary suffering for the sake of others is one of the three pillars of my philosophy of nonviolence. I call it "satyagrahi."

Oh yes, "satyagrahi." How did you come up with that name?

Sat, or Satya translates into the English word "truth." Tapasya means nonviolence and Ahi, or Ahimsa denotes self-suffering. Failure to grasp either of these three pillars of Satyagraha prohibits the full comprehension of this philosophy. Jesus exemplifies all three aspects of this philosophy in the composition of my undying faith in nonviolence which rules all my actions, worldly and temporal.

I understand that you kept a picture of Jesus hanging on the wall in your little hut. Is that right?

Gandhi: Yes, when I saw the black and white print of Jesus wearing only a loin cloth, my heart was deeply moved. It reminded me of the millions of poor people living in the Indian villages. It has a caption that reads, "He is our peace."

I understand that you have an affinity for the symbol of the cross as well. Is that right?

Gandhi: Yes, after returning from the 1931 Roundtable conference in London, I visited the

Vatican. It was there that I observed a life size version of the crucifix and was immediately struck with awe. I saw there, that many nations, like individuals, could be made whole. But only through the agony of the cross. There is no other way. Joy comes not by the infliction of pain on others, but the pain voluntarily borne by oneself.

Note: This preceding is a sample of the book, "Interview a Great Soul" which can be found at rationalbible.com. All donations and proceeds will go the Gandhi Farm Project. "Interview with a Great Soul" is made available for free however, to anyone who cannot afford to pay. The ultimate goal of Gandhi Farm will be to raise public awareness toward the association between self-reliance, empathy and world peace. Gandhi believed that an individual's primary objective should be the single-minded cultivation of one's "soul-force" through the realization of absolute truth, or "Satya" (for Gandhi, this was the essence of God). Gandhi Farm will allow individuals the opportunity to practice Gandhian ideals as such, as well as to share their own experiences, insights and permaculture techniques with likeminded others in a supportive, vegan and drug-free community environment.

Appendix B:
"What Jesus Means to Me" by Mahatma Gandhi

Although I have devoted a large part of my life to the study of religion and to discussion with religious leaders of all faiths, I know very well that I cannot but seem presumptuous in writing about Jesus Christ and trying to explain what he means to me. I do so only because my Christian friends have told me, on more than a few occasions, that for the very reason I am not a Christian and that (I shall quote their words exactly) "I do not accept Christ in the bottom of my heart as the only Son of God," it is impossible for me to understand the profound significance of his teachings, or to know and interpret the greatest source of spiritual strength that man has ever known.

Although this may or may not be true in my case, I have reasons to believe that it is an erroneous point of view. I believe that such an estimate is incompatible with the message that Jesus Christ gave to the world. For, he was certainly the highest example of one who wished to give everything, asking nothing in return, and not caring what creed might happen to be professed by the recipient. I am sure that if he were living here now among men, he would bless the lives of many who perhaps have never even heard his name, if only their lives embodied the virtues of which he was a living example on earth; the virtues of loving one's neighbor as oneself and of doing good and charitable works among one's fellowmen.

What, then, does Jesus mean to me? To me, he was one of the greatest teachers humanity has ever had. To his believers, he was God's only begotten Son.* Could the fact that I do or do not accept this belief make Jesus have any more or less influence in my life? Is all the grandeur of his teaching and of his doctrine to be forbidden to me? I cannot believe so.

To me, it implies a spiritual birth. My interpretation, in other words, is that in Jesus' own life is the key of his nearness to God; that he expressed, as no other could, the spirit and will of God. It is in this sense that I see him and recognize him as the Son of God.

The Spirit of Jesus

But I do believe that something of this spirit that Jesus exemplified in the highest measure, in its most profound human sense, does exist. I must believe this; if I did not believe it, I should be a sceptic; and to be a sceptic is to live a life that is empty and lacks moral content. Or, what is the same thing, to condemn the entire human race to a negative end.

It is true that there certainly is reason for skepticism when one observes the bloody butchery that European aggressors have unloosed, and when one thinks about the misery and suffering prevalent in every corner of the world, as well as the pestilence and famine that always follow, terribly and inevitably, upon war. In the face of this, how can one speak seriously of the Divine Spirit incarnate in man?

Because these acts of terror and murder offend the conscience of man; because man knows that they represent evil; because in the inner depths of his heart and of his mind, he deplores them. And because, moreover, when he does not go astray, misled by false teachings or corrupted by false leaders, man has within his breast an impulse for good and a compassion that is the spark of Divinity, and which some day, I believe, will burst forth into the full flower that is the hope of all mankind.

Jesus' Example

An example of this flowering may be found in the figure and in the life of Jesus. I refuse to believe that there now exists or has ever existed a person that has not made use of his example to lessen his sins, even though he may have done so without realizing it. The lives of all have, in some greater or lesser degree, been changed by his presence, his actions, and the words spoken by his divine voice.

I believe that it is impossible to estimate the merits of the various religions of the world, and, moreover, I believe that it is unnecessary and harmful even to attempt it. But each one of them, in my judgment, embodies a common motivating force: the desire to uplift man's life and give it purpose. And because the life of Jesus has the significance and the transcendency to which I have alluded, I believe that he belongs not solely to Christianity, but to the entire world; to all races and people, it matters little under what flag, name or doctrine they may work, profess a faith, or worship a God inherited from their ancestors.

Note: this article was published in the October, 1941 edition of "*The Modern Review*" and republished on mahatma.org.

Appendix C
"The Jesus I Love" A talk by Gandhi

Note: The following is a transcript of a talk given by Gandhi on a trip back to India after attending the Second Round Table Conference in London.

I shall tell you how, to an outsider like me, the story of Christ, as told in the New Testament, has struck. My acquaintance with the Bible began nearly forty-five years ago, and that was through the New Testament. I could not then take much interest in the Old Testament, which I had certainly read, if only to fulfill a promise I had made to a friend whom I happened to meet in a hotel. But when I came to the New Testament and the Sermon on the Mount, I began to understand the Christian teaching, and the teaching of the Sermon on the Mount echoed something I had learnt in childhood and something which seemed to be part of my being and which I felt was being acted up to in the daily life around me.

I say it seemed to be acted up to, meaning thereby that it was not necessary for my purpose that they were actually living the life. This teaching was non-retaliation, or non-resistance to evil. Of all the things I read, what remained with me forever was that Jesus came almost to give a new law — though he of course had said he had not come to give a new law, but tack something on to the old Mosaic Law.

Well, he changed it so that it became a new law — not an eye for an eye, and a tooth for a tooth, but to be ready to receive two blows when only one was given, and to go two miles when you were asked to go one. I said to myself, this is what one learns in one's childhood. Surely this is not Christianity. For all I had then been given to understand was that to be a Christian was to have a brandy bottle in one hand and beef in the other. The Sermon on the Mount, however, falsified the impression. As my contact with real Christians i.e., men living in fear of God, increased, I saw that the Sermon on the Mount was the whole of Christianity for him who wanted to live a Christian life. It is that Sermon which has endeared Jesus to me.

I may say that I have never been interested in a historical Jesus. I should not care if it was proved by someone that the man called Jesus never lived, and that what was narrated in the Gospels was a figment of the writer's imagination. For the Sermon on the Mount would still be true for me. Reading, therefore, the whole story in that light, it seems to me that Christianity has yet to be lived, unless one says that where there is boundless love and no idea of retaliation whatsoever, it is Christianity that lives. But then it surmounts all boundaries and book teaching. Then it is something indefinable, not capable of being preached to men, not capable of being transmitted from mouth to mouth, but from heart to heart. But Christianity is not commonly understood in that way.

Somehow, in God's providence, the Bible has been preserved from destruction by the Christians, so-called. The British and Foreign Bible Society has had it translated into many languages. All that may serve a real purpose in the time to come. Two thousand years in the life of a living faith may be nothing. For though we sang, "All glory to God on High and on the earth be peace," there seems to be today neither glory to God nor peace on earth. As long as it remains a hunger still unsatisfied, as long as Christ is not yet born, we have to look forward to Him. When real peace is established, we will not need demonstrations, but it will be echoed in our life, not only in individual life, but in corporate life.

Then we shall say Christ is born. That to me is the real meaning of the verse we have sung. Then we will not think of a particular day in the year as that of the birth of the Christ, but as an ever-recurring event which can be enacted in every life. And the more I think of fundamental religion, and the more I think of miraculous conceptions of so many teachers who have come down from age to age and clime to clime, the more I see that there is behind them the eternal truth that I have narrated. That needs no label or declaration. It consists in the living of life, never ceasing, ever progressing towards peace. When, therefore, one wishes "A Happy Christmas" without the meaning behind it, it becomes nothing more than an empty formula. And unless one wishes for peace for all life, one cannot wish for peace for oneself.

It is a self-evident axiom, like the axioms of Euclid, that one cannot have peace unless there is in one an intense longing for peace all around. You may certainly experience peace in the midst of strife, but that happens only when to remove strife you destroy your whole life, you crucify yourself.

And so, as the miraculous birth is an eternal event, so is the Cross an eternal event in this stormy life. Therefore, we dare not think of birth without death on the cross. Living Christ means a living Cross, without it life is a living death.

On that same Christmas day, Gandhi was urged by the Associated Press of America to issue a Holiday Greeting. His reply was as follows:

I have never been able to reconcile myself to the gaieties of the Christmas season. They have appeared to me to be so inconsistent with the life and teaching of Jesus."

"How I wish America could lead the way by devoting the season to a real moral stocktaking and emphasizing consecration to the service of mankind for which Jesus lived and died on the Cross."

Appendix D:
"Man's Greatest Force" by Gandhi

Non-violence is the greatest force man has been endowed with. Truth is the only goal he has. For God is none other than Truth. But Truth cannot be, never will be reached except through non-violence. That which distinguishes man from all other animals is his capacity to be non-violent. And he fulfills his mission only to the extent that he is non-violent and no more. He has no doubt many other gifts. But if they do not subserve the main purpose–the development of the spirit of non-violence in him–they but drag him down lower than the brute, a status from which he has only just emerged.

The cry for peace will be a cry in the wilderness, so long as the spirit of non-violence does not dominate millions of men and women. An armed conflict between nations horrifies us. But the economic war is no better than an armed conflict. This is like a surgical operation. An economic war is prolonged torture. And its ravages are no less terrible than those depicted in the literature on war properly so-called. We think nothing of the other because we are used to its deadly effects. Many of us in India shudder to see blood spilled. Many of us resent cow slaughter, but we think nothing of the slow torture through which by our greed we put our people and cattle. But because we are used to this lingering death, we think no more about it.

The movement against war is sound. I pray for its success. But I cannot help the gnawing fear that the movement will fail, if it does not touch the root of all evil– man's greed. Will America, England and the other great nations of the West continue to exploit the so called weaker or uncivilized races and hope to attain peace that the whole world is pining for? Or will Americans continue to prey upon one another, have commercial rivalries and yet expect to dictate peace to the world?

Not till the spirit is changed, can the form be altered. The form is merely an expression of the spirit within. We may succeed in seemingly altering the form but the alteration will be a mere make believe, if the spirit within remains unalterable. A whited sepulchre still conceals beneath it the rotting flesh and bone.

Far be it from me, to discount or under-rate the great effort that is being made in the West to kill the war-spirit. Mine is merely a word of caution as from a fellow seeker who has been striving in his own humble manner after the same thing, maybe in a different way, no doubt on a much smaller scale. But if the experiment demonstrably succeeds on the smaller field and, if those who are working on the larger field have not overtaken me, it will at least pave the way for a similar experiment on a large field. I observe in the limited field in which I find myself, that unless I can reach the hearts of men and women, I am able to do nothing. I observe further that so long as the spirit of hate persists in some shape or other, it is impossible to establish peace or to gain our freedom by peaceful effort. We cannot love one another, if we hate Englishmen.

We cannot love the Japanese and hate Englishmen. We must either let the law of love rule us through and through or not at all. Love among ourselves based on hatred of others breaks down under the slightest pressure. The fact is, such love is never real love. It is an armed peace. And so it will be in this great movement in the West against War. War will only be stopped when the conscience of mankind has become sufficiently elevated to recognize the undisputed supremacy of the Law of Love in all the walks of life. Some say this will never come to pass. I shall retain the faith till the end of my earthly existence that it shall come to pass.

Appendix E:
"The Doctrine of the Sword" by M.K. Gandhi

In this age of the rule of brute force, it is almost impossible for anyone to believe that anyone else could possibly reject the law of the final supremacy of brute force. And so I receive anonymous letters advising me that I must not interfere with the progress of non-co-operation even though popular violence may break out. Others come to me and assuming that secretly I must be plotting violence, inquire when the happy moment for declaring open violence will arrive. They assure me that the English will never yield to anything but violence secret or open. Yet others, I am informed, believe that I am the most rascally person living in India because I never give out my real intention and that they have not a shadow of a doubt that I believe in violence just as much as most people do. Such being the hold that the doctrine of the sword has on the majority of mankind, and as success of non-co-operation depends principally on absence of violence during its pendency and as my views in this matter affect the conduct of a large number of people, I am anxious to state them as clearly as possible.

I do believe that where there is only a choice between cowardice and violence I would advise violence. Thus when my eldest son asked me what he should have done, had he been present when I was almost fatally assaulted in 1908, whether he should have run away and seen me killed or whether he should have used his physical force which he could and wanted to use, and defended me, I told him that it was his duty to defend me even by using violence.

Hence it was that I took part in the Boer War, the so-called Zulu rebellion and the late War. Hence also do I advocate training in arms for those who believe in the method of violence. I would rather have India resort to arms in order to defend her honor than that she should in a cowardly manner become or remain a helpless witness to her own dishonor. But I believe that non-violence is infinitely superior to violence, forgiveness is more manly than punishment. Forgiveness adorns a soldier. But abstinence is forgiveness only when proceed from a helpless creature. A mouse hardly forgives a cat when it allows itself to be torn to pieces by her. I, therefore, appreciate the sentiment of those who cry out for the condign punishment of General Dyer and his like. They would tear him to pieces if they could. But I do not believe India to be helpless. I do not believe myself to be a helpless creature. Only I want to use India's and my strength for a better purpose.

Let me not be misunderstood. Strength does not come from physical capacity. It comes from an indomitable will. An average Zulu is any way more than a match for an average Englishman in bodily capacity.

But he flees from an English boy, because he fears the boys revolver or those who will use it for him. He fears death and is nerveless in spite of his burly figure. We in India may in a moment realize that one hundred thousand Englishmen need not frighten three hundred million human beings. A definite forgiveness would therefore mean a definite recognition of our strength. With enlightened forgiveness must come a mighty wave of strength in us, which would make it impossible for a Dyer and a Frank Johnson to heap affront upon Indias devoted head. It matters little to me that for the moment I do not drive my point home. We feel too downtrodden not to be angry and revengeful. But I must not refrain from saying that India can gain more by waiving the right of punishment. We have better work to do, a better mission to deliver to the world.

I am not a visionary. I claim to be a practical idealist. The religion of non-violence is not meant merely for the rishis and saints. It is meant for the common people as well. Non-violence is the law of our species as violence is the law of the brute. The spirit lies dormant in the brute and he knows no law but that of physical might. The dignity of man requires obedience to a higher law to the strength of the spirit. I have therefore ventured to place before India the ancient law of self-sacrifice. For satyagraha and its off-shoots, non-co-operation and civil resistance, are nothing but new names for the law of suffering.

The rishis, who discovered the law of non-violence in the midst of violence, were greater geniuses than Newton. They were themselves greater warriors than Wellington. Having themselves known the use of arms, they realized their uselessness and taught a weary world that its salvation lay not through violence but through non-violence. Non-violence in its dynamic condition means conscious suffering. It does not mean meek submission to the will of the evildoer, but it means the putting of ones soul against the will of the tyrant. Working under this law of our being, it is possible for a single individual to defy the whole might of an unjust empire to save his honour, his religion, his soul and lay the foundation for that empires fall or its regeneration.

And so I am not pleading for India to practise non-violence because it is weak. I want her to practise non-violence being conscious of her strength and power. No training in arms is required for realization of her strength. We seem to need it because we seem to think that we are but a lump of flesh. I want India to recognize that she has a soul that cannot perish and that can rise triumphant above every physical weakness and defy the physical combination of whole world. What is the meaning of Rama, a mere human being, with his host of monkeys, pitting himself against the insolent strength of ten-headed Ravana surrounded in supposed safety by the raging waters on all sides of Lanka?

Does it not mean the conquest of physical might by spiritual strength? However, being a practical man, I do not wait till India recognizes the practicability of the spiritual life in the political world. India considers herself to be powerless and paralysed before the machineguns, the tanks and the aeroplanes of the

English. And she takes up non-co-operation out of her weakness. It must still serve the same purpose, namely, bring her delivery from the crushing weight of British injustice if a sufficient number of people practise it.

I isolate this non-co-operation from Sinn Feinism, for, it is so conceived as to be incapable of being offered side by side with violence. But I invite even the school of violence to give this peaceful non-co-operation a trial. It will not fail through its inherent weakness. It may fail because of poverty of response. Then will be the time for real danger. The high-souled men, who are unable to suffer national humiliation any longer, will want to vent their wrath. They will take to violence. So far as I know, they must perish without delivering themselves or their country from the wrong. If India takes up the doctrine of the sword, she may gain momentary victory. Then India will cease to be pride of my heart. I am wedded to India because I owe my all to her. I believe absolutely that she has a mission for the world. She is not to copy Europe blindly. India's acceptance of the doctrine of the sword will be the hour of my trial. I hope I shall not be found wanting. My religion has no geographical Limits.

If I have a living faith in it, it will transcend my love for India herself. My life is dedicated to service of India through the religion of non-violence which I believe to be the root of Hinduism. Meanwhile I urge those who distrust me, not to disturb the even working of the struggle that has just commenced, by inciting to violence in the belief that I want violence. I detest secrecy as a sin. Let them give non-violent non-co-operation a trial and they will find that I had no mental reservation whatsoever.

Appendix F:
Gandhi's Speech at Kingsley Hall (1931)

There is an indefinable mysterious power that pervades everything. I feel it, though I do not see it. It is this unseen power which makes itself felt and yet defies all proof because it is so unlike all that I perceive through my senses. It transcends the senses.

But it is possible to reason out the existence of God to an [inaudible] exchange. Even in ordinary affairs we know that people do not know who rules, or why, and how he rules. And yet they know that there is a power that certainly rules. In my tour last year in Mysore I met many poor villagers and I found upon inquiry that they did not know who ruled Mysore. They simply said some God ruled it. If the knowledge of these poor people was so limited about their ruler, I, who am infinitely lesser in respect to God than they to their ruler need not be surprised if I do not realize the presence of God, the King of kings.

Nevertheless I do feel as the poor villagers felt about Mysore, that there is orderliness in the universe. There is an unalterable law governing everything and every being that exists or lives. It is not a blind law, for no blind law can govern the conduct of living beings. And thanks to the marvelous researches of Sir J.C. Bose, it can now be proved that even matter is life.

That law then which governs all life is God. Law and the Lawgiver are one. I may not deny the law or the

Lawgiver because I know so little about it or him, just as my denial or ignorance of the existence of an earthly power will avail me nothing. Even so, my denial of God and his law will not liberate me from its operation. Whereas, humble and mute acceptance of divine authority makes life's journey easier even as the acceptance of earthly rule makes life under it easier.

I do dimly perceive that whilst everything around me is ever dying, ever guiding, there is underlying all that change a living power that is changeless, that holds all together; that creates, dissolves, and recreates. That informing power of spirit is God. And since nothing else that I see merely through the senses can or will persist, he alone is.

And if this power is benevolent or malevolent, I see it as purely benevolent. For, I can see that in the midst of death, life persists. In the midst of untruth, truth persists. In the midst of darkness, light persists. Hence I gather that God is life, truth, light. He is love. He is the supreme good. But, he is no God who merely satisfies the intellect, if he ever does. God to be God must rule the heart and transform it. He must express himself in ever smallest act of his [goodery?]. This can only be done through a definite realization more real than the fives senses can ever prove use.

Sense perceptions can be and often are false and deceptive however real they may appear to us. Where there is realization outside the senses it is [imperial?], it is proved not by extreme extraneous evidence, but in the transformed conduct and character of those who have felt the real presence of God within. Such testimony is to be found in the experiences of an unbroken line of prophets and sages in all countries and climes. To reject this evidence is to deny oneself. This realization is preceded by an immovable faith. He who would in his own person, test the fact of God's presence can do so by a living faith.

And since faith itself cannot be proved by extraneous evidence, the safest course is to believe in the moral government of the world and therefore in the supremacy of the moral law, the law of truth and love. Exercise of faiths will be the safest where there is the clear determination summarily to reject all that is contrary to truth and love.

I confess that I have no argument to convince through reason. Faith transcends reason. All that I can advise is not to attempt the impossible.

References and Suggested Reading:

Abbott, L. (1921). What Christianity Means to Me: A Spiritual Autobiography. Macmillan.

Abel M (2005). Glimpses of Indian National Movement. ICFAI Books.

Aesop's fables (2002). Oxford University Press,

Ali, S. A. (1981). History of the Saracens.

Ali, S. A. (2010). The spirit of Islam: A history of the evolution and ideals of Islam. Cosimo, Inc..

Andrews, C. F. (1920). Mahatma Gandhi's Ideas.

Andrews, C. F. (1932). What I owe to Christ. Hodder & Stoughton.

Andrews, C. F. (2008) [1930]. "VII – The Teaching of Ahimsa". Mahatma Gandhi's Ideas Including Selections from His Writings. Pierides Press.

Andrews, C. F., & khān bahādur Nazīr Ahmad. (1929). Zaka ullah of Delhi (pp. 97-97). Cambridge: W. Heffer & Sons.

Arnold, E. (1892). The Light of Asia, Or, The Great Renunciation. Roberts.

Aurobindo, S., & Ghose, A. (2000). Essays on the Gita. SriAurobindoAshram Publication Dept.

Beitzel, T. (2013). Virtue in the Nonviolence of William James and Gandhi. International Journal on World Peace, 30(3), C1.

Bell, D. C., & Bell, A. M. (1902). Bell's Standard Elocutionist: Principles and Exercises... Hodder and Stoughton.

Bellamy, E. (1970). Equality. 1897.

Bennett, L. (1992). What manner of man: A biography of Martin Luther King, Jr. Johnson Publishing Company, Inc..

Besant, A. W. (1890). Why I Became a Theosophist. " The Path" Office.

Blavatsky, H. P. (1930). The Key to Theosophy by HP Blavatsky. Theosophy Trust Books.

Blount, G. (1903). A new crusade. Simple Life Press.

Böhme, J. (1901). Dialogues on the supersensual life. Methuen & Company.

Boodberg, P. A. (1951). Tolstoy and China: A Critical Analysis. Philosophy East and West, 1(3), 64-76.

Brailsford, H. N. (1931). Rebel India. New York: New Republic.

Brierley, J. (1906). Religion and expérience. James Clarke.

Buck, P. S. (1931). The good earth (Vol. 1). Simon and Schuster.

Buckle, H. T. (1906). History of civilization in England (Vol. 2). D. Appleton.

Bühler, G. (Ed.). (1886). The laws of Manu (Vol. 25). Clarendon Press.

Bunyan, J., & Walton, I. (1909). Pilgrim's progress (Vol. 15). PF Collier & son.

Bureau, P. (1925). Towards moral bankruptcy. Constable.

Butler, J. (1878). The analogy of religion, natural and revealed, to the constitution and course of nature. George Bell and Sons.

Carlyle, T. (1832). Boswell's Life of Johnson. Fraser's Magazine, 5, 379-413.

Carlyle, T. (1838). Memoirs of the Life of Scott. London and Westminster Review, 6.

Carlyle, T. (1872). Past and Present (1843). Chapman and Hall.

Carlyle, T. (1880). Life of Robert Burns. American book exchange.

Carlyle, T. (1881). The French revolution: a history. American Book Exchange.

Carpenter, E. (1904). From Adam's peak to Elephanta: sketches in Ceylon and India. EP Dutton.

Carpenter, E. (Ed.). (1921). Civilisation, Its Cause and Cure: And Other Essays. Scribner.

Carus, P. (2012). The Gospel of Buddha (Extended Annotated Edition). Jazzybee Verlag.

Chao, L. I. U. (2008). The Spirit Search of Tolstoy and Confucianism, Taoism and Mohism. Journal of Baoding University, 1, 020.

Confucius. (1958). The wisdom of Confucius. L. Yutang (Ed.). Michael Joseph.

Coomaraswamy, A. (2006). Essays in national idealism. Hesperides Press.

Cox, G. W. (1898). The Crusades. C. Scribner's sons.

Dalton, Dennis, ed. (1996). Mahatma Gandhi: Selected Political Writings. Hackett Publishing.

Das, B. (2007). The Science of Peace. Mill Press.

Drummond, H. (1893). Natural law in the spiritual world. Hodder and Stoughton.

Drummond, H. (1998). The greatest thing in the world. Bridge Logos Foundation.

Duncan, Ronald, ed. (May 2011). Selected Writings of Mahatma Gandhi. Literary Licensing, LLC.

Ellsberg, R. (Ed.). (2013). Gandhi on Christianity. Orbis Books.

Epictetus, & Stoneman, R. (1995). The discourses of Epictetus. C. Gill (Ed.). JM Dent.

Epictetus. (1928). The discourses as reported by Arrian, the manual, and fragments. Heinemann.

Feuerbach, L. (2004). The essence of Christianity. Barnes & Noble Publishing.

Fingarette, H. (1998). Confucius: The secular as sacred. Waveland Press.

Foxe, J. (1989). Foxe's christian martyrs of the world. Barbour Publishing.

Gandhi, M. K.(2008). My experiments with truth: An autobiography. Jaico Publishing House.

Gandhi, M. K. (1960). Non-Voilence In Peace And War.

Gandhi, M. K. (2001). Non-violent resistance. Courier Corporation.

Gandhi, M. K.; Fischer, Louis (2002). Louis Fischer, ed. The Essential Gandhi: An Anthology of His Writings on His Life, Work and Ideas. Vintage Books.

Gandhi, M. K. (1928). "Drain Inspector's Report". The United States of India **5** (6,7,8): 3–4.

Gandhi, M. K. (1928). Satyagraha in South Africa (in Gujarati) (1 ed.). Ahmedabad: Navajivan Publishing House. Translated by Valji G. Desai Free online access at Wikilivres.ca (1/e). Pdfs from Gandhiserve (3/e) & Yann Forget (hosted by Arvind Gupta) (1/e).

Gandhi, M.K. (1990). Desai, Mahadev H., ed. Autobiography: The Story of My Experiments With Truth. Mineola, N.Y.: Dover.

Gandhi, M. K. (1994). The Collected Works of Mahatma Gandhi. Publications Division, Ministry of Information and Broadcasting, Govt. of India. (100 volumes). Free online access from Gandhiserve.

Gandhi, Rajmohan (2007). Mohandas: True Story of a Man, His People. Penguin Books Limited.

Gier, N. F. (2001). Confucius, Gandhi and the aesthetics of virtue. Asian Philosophy, 11(1), 41-54.

Gopal, B. R. (1983). Sri Ramanuja in Karnataka: an epigraphical study. Sundeep Prakashan.

Guha, Ramachandra (2 October 2013). "1. Middle Cast, Middle Rank". Gandhi Before India. Penguin Books Limited. Jack, Homer A., ed. (1994). The Gandhi Reader: A Source Book of His Life and Writings. Grove Press.

Haeckel, E. (1903). The evolution of man: a popular exposition of the principal points of human ontogeny and phylogeny (Vol. 1). D. Appleton.

Hofstede, G., & Bond, M. H. (1988). The Confucius connection: From cultural roots to economic growth. Organizational dynamics, 16(4), 5-21.

Hugo, V. (1874). Ninety-three (Vol. 1). Harper & brothers.

Hugo, V. M. (1862). Les misérables (Vol. 3).

Johnson, Richard L. and Gandhi, M. K. (2006). Gandhi's Experiments With Truth: Essential Writings by and about Mahatma Gandhi. Lexington Books.

Just, A. (1912). Return to nature. G. Routledge & Sons, Limited.

Kidd, B. (1915). Social evolution. Macmillan.

King III, M. L. (2008). The Words of Martin Luther King, Jr. Newmarket Press.

King, M. L. (1960). Pilgrimage to nonviolence (p. 135). Fellowship Publications.

King, M. L. (1992). I have a dream: Writings and speeches that changed the world. J. M. Washington (Ed.). HarperSanFrancisco.

King, M., & Mayor, F. (1999). Mahatma Gandhi and Martin Luther King Jr: the power of nonviolent action. Paris: Unesco.

Kingsford, A. (1999). Clothed with the Sun. NuVision Publications, LLC.

Kohn, L., & LaFargue, M. (Eds.). (1998). Lao-tzu and the Tao-te-ching. SUNY Press.

LaFargue, M., & Pas, J. (1998). On Translating the Tao-te-ching. Lao-tzu and the.

Long, A. A. (2002). Epictetus: A Stoic and Socratic Guide to Life: A Stoic and Socratic Guide to Life. Oxford University Press.

Long, A. A. (2006). From Epicurus to Epictetus: studies in Hellenistic and Roman philosophy.

Marett, R. R. (1909). The tabu-mana Formula as a Minimum Definition of Religion. Archiv für Religionswissenschaft, 12, 186-194.

Marx, K. (2015). Capital A Critical Analysis Of Capitalist Production, Vol. 1.

Mauss, M. (1972). A General Theory of Magic, trans. Robert Brain. London, UK and Boston, MA: Routledge and Kegan Paul Ltd.

McLaughlin, E. T. (1974). Ruskin and Gandhi.

Mittal, S. K. (2004). Jainism and Mahatma Gandhi. India's medieval and modern past, 3, 169.

Modi, P. M. (Ed.). (1955). The Bhagavadgita: A Fresh Approach:(With Special Reference to Sankaracarya's Bhasya). India.

Moulton, J. H. (1913). Early Zoroastrianism: Lectures. Williams and Norgate.

Narang, G. C. (1960). Transformation of Sikhism. New Book Society of India.

Nayak, P. K. GANDHI AND CONFLICT RESOLUTION: A RETHINKING. SPECIAL ISSUE ON GANDHI, 1.

Oates, S. B. (1998). Let the trumpet sound: A life of Martin Luther King, Jr. Canongate Books.

Page, K. (1923). War; Its Causes Consequences and Cure. H. Doran Company.

Parekh, B. C. (2010). Gandhi. Sterling Publishing Company, Inc..

Parel, Anthony J., ed. (2009). Gandhi: "Hind Swaraj" and Other Writings Centenary Edition. Cambridge University Press.

Parker, T. (1876). The Collected Works of Theodore Parker: A discourse of matter pertaining to religion (Vol. 1). Trübner.

Pascal, B., & Havet, E. (1852). Pensées. Dezobry et E. Magdeleine.

Pierson, A. T. (1886). " Many infallible proofs": the evidences of Christianity. FH Revell company.

Ramsey, P. (1950). Basic christian ethics. Westminster John Knox Press.

Rao, M. M. NGUGI'S GRAIN OF WHEAT: A QUEST FOR MEANING. Ind-Africana, 4(1), 59.

Robertson, F. W. (1860). Sermons on St. Paul's Epistles to the Corinthians: Delivered at Trinity Chapel, Brighton. Ticknor and Fields.

Robertson, F. W. (1872). Expository Lectures on St. Paul's Epistles to the Corinthians: Delivered at Brighton: By the Late Rev. Frederick W. Robertson. Henry S. King and Company.

Robertson, F. W. (1874). Sermons preached at Trinity chapel, Brighton (Vol. 2). JR Osgood.

Ruskin, J. (1901). Unto this last: Four essays on the first principles of political economy (Vol. 623). George Allen.

Russell, G. W. (1920). The candle of vision. Macmillan.

Salt, H. S. (1886). plea for vegetarianism.

Salter, W. M. (1889). Ethical religion. Roberts.

Shaw, G. B. (1946). Man and superman. Penguin.

Somerville, J., & Santoni, R. (2012). Social and political philosophy: Readings from Plato to Gandhi. Anchor.

Stoudt, J. J. (1947). Jacob Boehme's The Way to Christ: in a New Translation.

Swami, V. (1973). Raja-yoga or conquering the internal nature. Advaita Ashrama, Calcutta.

Swift, J. (2005). Gulliver's travels. Oxford University Press.

Tagore, R. (2000). Gitanjali. Courier Corporation.

Taylor, T. F. (1909). The Fallacy of Speed. AC Fifield.

Tennyson, A. T. B. (1907). The Works of Alfred, Lord Tennyson, Poet Laureate. Macmillan.

The Golden Book of Tagore. Rammohun Library & Free Reading Room, 1990.

The Upanishads. Oxford University Press, 1900.

Thoreau, H. D. (2014). Life without principle. Netlancers Inc.

Thoreau, Henry David. Civil Disobedience and Other Essays (The Collected Essays of Henry David Thoreau). Digireads. com Publishing, 2010.

Tilak, B. G. (1893). The Orion. Poona (4th ed., Poona 1955).

Tilak, B. G. (1965). The Hindu philosophy of life, ethics and religion.

Timperley, H. J. (Ed.). (1938). What war means: the Japanese terror in China; a documentary record (Vol. 86). V. Gollancz, ltd..

Todd, Anne M. (2009). Mohandas Gandhi. Infobase Publishing.

357

Tolstoy, L. (1903). Essays and letters.

Tolstoy, L. (1908). Letter to a Hindoo. Letter to a Hindoo: Taraknath Das, Leo Tolostoy and Mahatma Gandhi,(ed.) Christian Bartolf. Berlin: Gandhi-Informations-Zentrum.

Tolstoy, L. (1927). The kingdom of God is within you. Editions Artisan Devereaux.

Tolstoy, L. (1936). Twenty-three tales (Vol. 72). H. Milford, Oxford university press.

Tolstoy, L. (1937). The first step. Recollections and Essays, 90-135.

Tolstoy, L. (1962). What is art?: and essays on art (Vol. 331). Reprint Services Corp.

Tolstoy, L. (1967). Letter to Ernest Howard Crosby. Tolstoy's Writings on Civil Disobedience and Non-Violence, trans. A. Maude, 181-190.

Tolstoy, L. (1975). The Inevitable Revolution. Trans, by R. Sampson. Housmans.

Tolstoy, L. (1987). Patriotism, or Peace?. Tolstoy's Writings on Civil Disobedience and Non-Violence, 106-107.

Tolstoy, L. (1996). Confession. WW Norton & Company.

Tolstoy, L. (2010). The death of Ivan Ilyich and other stories. Random House.

Tolstoy, L. (2012). The gospel in brief. Andrews UK Limited.

Tolstoy, L. N. (1882). Ivan the Fool. Best Classic Books.

Tolstoy, L. N. (2004). What Shall We Do Then?.

Tolstoy, L. N. (2009). What I believe. Cosimo, Inc..

Tolstoy, L., & Maude, A. (1951). The Gospel in Brief, and What i Believe. Oxford U. P.

Verne, J. (1909). Dropped from the Clouds. Dent.

Wadia, A. S. N. (1913). The Message of Zoroaster. JM Dent.

Wadia, A. S. N. (1938). The Message of Buddha (Vol. 6). Dent.

Wadia, S. (Ed.). (1940). The Aryan Path (Vol. 11). Theosophy Company (India), Limited.

Watters, T. (1870). Lao-tzu: A Study in Chinese Philosophy. Printed at the" China mail" Office.

Wellington, W. S. (1922). Some influences of the crusades on the architecture of Western Europe. University of California. May.

Whately, R. (1868). Bacon's essays with annotations.

White, F. T., Tudor, O. D., Hare, J. I. C., & Wallace, H. B. (1849). A selection of leading cases in equity: with notes (Vol. 1). T. & JW Johnson.

Wilde, O. (2003). Complete Works of Oscar Wilde Vol 9. Aubrey Durkin.

Williams, H. (1883). Ethics of Diet. F. Pitman.

Wordsworth, W. (1869). The poetical works of William Wordsworth. E. Moxon, Son, and Company.

Note: Books dated before 1948 were highly influential on Gandhi. These works and many more are available for free viewing or download at rationalbible.com. Other informational resources on Mahatma Gandhi can be found from the following organizations.:

Bombay Sarvodaya Mandal - Gandhi Book Centre, Mumbai
299, Tardeo Road, Nana Chowk, Bombay 400007 India
Tel:91-22-2387 2061
Email: info@mkgandhi.org

Gandhi Research Foundation, Jalgaon
Jain Agri Park, Jain Hills, Shirsoli Road,
Jalgaon, 425 001 MH, India
Tel. +91-257-2260 011
www.gandhifoundation.net

M.K. Gandhi Institute for Nonviolence
929 S. Plymouth Ave.
Rochester, New York 14608
Phone 585-463-3266

Honorable Mentions:

I would like to mention two people whose works inspired me throughout the writing of this book, The first is Gary Yourofsky, a radical animal rights activist. The second is Arun Gandhi, a social activist and fifth grandson of Mohandas K. "Mahatma" Gandhi. I hope you'll support their causes as you have mine. Thank you and don't forget to check out the free resources at rationalbible.com!

Gandhi, A. (1969). A Patch of White. [Bombay]: Thackers.

Gandhi, A. (1998). Forgotten Woman: The Untold Story of Kastur, Wife of Mahatma Gandhi. Ozark Mountain Publishing (AR).

Gandhi, A. (1999). World Without Violence: Can Gandhi's Vision Become Reality?. MK Gandhi Institute for Nonviolence.

Gandhi, A. (2003). Legacy of love: My education in the path of nonviolence. North Bay Books.

Gandhi, A. (2013). The Sincerity of Purpose: Sustainability and World Peace. In Practicing Sustainability (pp. 45-49). Springer New York.

Yourofsky, G. (2006). Gary Yourofsky Speaks on Animal Cruelty.

Yourofsky, G. (2008). What They Never Told You.

Brian Whaley Events

Brian Whaley is available for speaking engagements and author appearances. For assembly presentations at schools, Brian shares what inspired him to become a writer, and brings history to life by showing students photos from the time periods discussed. He obtained his undergraduate degree in Management & Human Relations at Trevecca Nazarene University in Nashville, Tennessee. Brian also holds a Master's Degree in Industrial - Organizational Psychology from Austin Peay University in Clarksville.

For more information, please contact:

Brian Whaley

Phone: (877) 736-9963

Email: media@brianwhaley.com